WORKAHOLICS

To Jim Wyngaarden

President,

    Workaholics Anonymous

With best wishes for a busy

new year in '81

    Regards,

        David Purack

Christmas 1980

WORKAHOLICS
Living With
Them,
Working With
Them

Marilyn Machlowitz, Ph.D.

ADDISON-WESLEY PUBLISHING COMPANY

Reading, Massachusetts
Menlo Park, California   London   Amsterdam
Don Mills, Ontario   Sydney

Portions of the material in this book previously appeared in:

The New York Times, October 3, 1976 and July 17, 1977.
Copyright© 1976 and 1977 The New York Times
Company.

Across the Board, October, 1977 and January, 1979.
Copyright © 1977 and 1979 The Conference Board Inc.

Working Woman, May, 1978.
Copyright© 1978 Hal Publications Inc.

Library of Congress Cataloging in Publication Data

Machlowitz, Marilyn M   1952–
    Workaholics, Living With Them, Working With Them
    Bibliography: p. 161
    Includes index.
    1. Work—Psychological aspects.   I. Title.
HF5548.8.M19   155.2′32   79-25308
ISBN 0-201-04614-8
ISBN 0-201-04613-X pbk.

ISBN 0-201-04613-X-P
ISBN 0-201-04614-8-H

ABCDEFGHIJ-DO-89876543210

Acknowledgments

I am grateful for the expertise, enthusiasm, and effort of Professor J. Richard Hackman, who served as advisor for both my master's thesis and doctoral dissertation. Our most vehement argument during my years at Yale concerned the question of whether he was a workaholic. (He denies it.) I am also indebted to additional members of Yale's faculty—particularly Rosabeth Moss Kanter, Seymour B. Sarason, Daniel J. Levinson, and Faye Crosby—for their part in guiding my research.

The 100 workaholics I studied were more than mere "research subjects." Their intelligent and articulate insights invariably suggested additional areas for investigation. I am also indebted to one additional workaholic, Robin Denrich, who typed multiple drafts of this manuscript.

Marylin Bender, then of *The New York Times*, Clay Felker, then of *Esquire*, Lewis Bergman of *Across the Board*, and Kate Rand Lloyd of *Working Woman* published the articles that led to this book. I owe a big debt to them and to Ann Dilworth, Warren Stone, Anne Eldridge, and Martha Drumm of Addison-Wesley.

My friends provided the distractions and diversions without which this book might have been finished earlier—and the encouragement without which it might not have been finished at all.

Nothing I could write about my family—particularly my parents—would adequately express my appreciation and my admiration. It is to them that this book is dedicated.

New York City   M. M. M.
January 1980

Special Thanks

The people cited in the following list were among those I interviewed, either in person, over the telephone, or by mail, and were kind enough to grant permission to attribute some of their remarks in the book.

Monica Bauer	Sally MacKinnon
Jay Bennett	John Meeks
Frank Berger	Leo Miller
Stuart Berger	Jeno Paulucci
Alan Chodos	Harvey Pitt
Denton Cooley	Shirley Polykoff
Laurel Cutler	Steven Poses
Helen DeRosis	Maurice Prout
Peter Drucker	William Proxmire
Eileen Ford	Gilda Radner
Milton Glaser	Gerard Roche
Shelly Gross	Jay Rohrlich
Andrew Hart	Lee Salk
Florence Haseltine	Jessica Savitch
Beverly Holding	Darrell Sifford
Hal Holding	Neil Simon
Louis L'Amour	Lawrence Susser
George Lang	Alexandra Symonds
Jack Lenor Larsen	Dick Vermeil
George Lois	Elizabeth Whelan

Introduction

I first heard the word "workaholic" when my father called me one. At the time (1971), I had just finished my freshman year at Princeton and was about to begin working at *three* summer jobs. My father, who would have preferred to see me spend the summer backpacking around Europe, was less than pleased. "You know what you are?" he said, "A workaholic."

He had no idea that the term he tossed off would become the subject of my master's thesis, my doctoral dissertation, and this book. But the word stuck with me. As I completed college and started graduate school at Yale, I saw professors and deans who seemed to work extremely hard without the narrowness or unhappiness that was *supposed* to accompany such devotion to duty. Later, as I began to consult for corporations in New York, I met executives who were undoubtedly workaholics, but who doubtlessly enjoyed themselves. One, a banker, circled the globe several times a year presenting financial seminars and not incidentally securing countless clients for his employer. At the same time, he was a regular guest on the television show, "Wall Street Week," and a widely published author. Yet his energy and enthusiasm were ever-present; his sense of humor, effervescent.

These observations led me to question the negative stereotype associated with the word "workaholic." Having studied both clinical and industrial psychology, I combined multiple research techniques to try to set the record straight. I wanted to find out what was wrong—and more important, what was *right*—with being a workaholic.

But in order to study workaholics, I first had to find some. It wasn't easy. Although associations such as Alcoholics Anonymous and Gamblers Anonymous abound, there is no "Workaholics Anonymous." (Nor, as shall be shown, should there be.) The lack of a specific population to sample or any single source of subjects forced me to find other ways of tracking them down.

One way with obvious appeal would have been to watch them at work—in other words, to catch workaholics in the act. Alfred Eisenstaedt, the famous *Life* photographer, captured then Secretary of State Henry Kissinger with a phone at one ear, a pen in one hand, and his lap loaded with reading material while sitting in a barber chair. Eisenstaedt told *Time*, "I wanted to take it there because other people snooze or do nothing when their hair is being cut. I'd been told Kissinger was busy all the time." Similarly, I thought about standing outside office buildings to see who entered at 6 A.M. or emerged at 10 P.M. but ultimately decided against it: I didn't have the nerve.

But an almost unprecedented and, I hope, unlikely to be repeated opportunity to observe workaholics occurred the day of the 1977 New York blackout, when I meandered around Manhattan's midtown business district. There I found hundreds of people who had gone to work despite then Mayor Beame's and Governor Carey's radio requests to stay home.

A second way in which I found workaholics was by scanning daily papers and weekly magazines for references to "seventy-hour work weeks," "eighteen-hour days," and the like. For instance, one article I clipped from *People* included this description of the daily pattern of Isaac Asimov, the well-known science fiction writer:

> Up at 6 A.M., after four or five hours' sleep, he consumes *The New York Times* and a hearty breakfast. By 8 A.M., he is battering away at his IBM. Asimov admits if he spends three hours away from his typewriter, he has an anxiety attack.

The third source of subjects was simply the recommendations of those I know and those I interviewed. Some of the latter group were so eager to assist me that they started going through their Rolodexes spontaneously. They would suggest names ("You know who you should really talk with?") even before being asked.

As hard as it was to find workaholics, interviewing them was even worse. Since some were too busy working to take the time to talk, interviews had to be scheduled weeks or even months in advance. When anyone said something to the effect of "I'll be out of town most of January; how about February?" I interpreted such statements more as grist for the mill than as a reluctance to be interviewed.

This is not to say that I got to interview everyone I approached. When I asked Alex Lewyt, the vacuum cleaner magnate, for an appointment after reading an article outlining his work habits, he told me, "You've got to believe the article. I'm too busy working."

When interviews proved impossible or geographically infeasible, I resorted to mail questionnaires and telephone interviews. (Many people put me on speaker phones, keeping their hands free to work or, in one case, to eat.) Not every questionnaire was completed or returned. The one I sent to Robert Strauss, now chairman of President Carter's re-election campaign, came back unanswered. In an accompanying letter an aide explained, "I have survived the last six or so years with Strauss by keeping things like this off his desk and out of his hands—that being one of the ways in which he is able to get a lot of things done."

Interviewing workaholics required incredible flexibility. I met with them whenever and wherever they wished, seven days a week, in cars, cabs, and limousines. I found that when they said, "First thing in the morning," they usually meant 7:30, not 9:00.

Their tight schedules sometimes required talking on the run. A New York television reporter permitted me to accompany him on an assignment. As he raced through red lights, I tried to keep talking and taping. I followed him into City Hall and found myself in the midst of Edward Koch's first press conference as Mayor of New York. One man remembered mid-interview that it was time to attend his daughter's school Christmas pageant. I continued interviewing him in a cab on the way to her school, watched the play, and completed the interview during the cab ride back to his office.

As a group, they were not easy to interview. Many seemed assured to the point of arrogance. Such arrogance, however, was no indication of the people's actual importance. The president of a major utility company asked his secretaries to hold all calls while we spoke. In contrast, a minor publishing figure not only accepted endless phone calls, but placed several more.

Many were most impatient. One man told me, "If you weren't prepared—which you are—and I had to wait twenty seconds between questions, I'd ask you to leave." Others were rather contemptuous. Once I could not begin an interview because the tape recorder's ten-foot cord was too short to reach any outlet in one man's enormous office. He looked at me with undisguised disdain and said, "*I* always carry an extension cord." Thereafter, so did I.

Occasionally, the workaholics themselves were not difficult to deal with but their co-workers were. When I interviewed "Saturday Night Live" star Gilda Radner, a co-star sat there listening to Gilda and glaring at me, seemingly annoyed at not being interviewed too. On another appointment, this time with a corporate president, the firm's public relations chief insisted on sitting in and then persisted in answering my questions before his boss could open his mouth.

Several confirmed their workaholism by trying to take care of paperwork while we spoke. But most quickly turned their complete attention to the interview. The topic was clearly of considerable concern to them. As one said, "I'm doing this more for me than for you."

Others seemed to welcome the opportunity to talk about their work. Most gave me detailed descriptions of the intricacies and, in one case, illegalities involved in what they did. My questions seemed to make them remember long forgotten adolescent ambitions and to force them to confront and acknowledge—perhaps for the first time—aspects of their attitudes toward work. As one said, "I'm saying things I don't think I would have admitted before." The slight self-consciousness that followed some revelations and reminiscences indicated how candid they had been. Some wondered aloud, "Why am I telling you this?" or recalled, "Gee, I haven't told anyone about that in years."

Such candor was crucial, especially in those cases where the individuals themselves were to serve as the only source of information and insight. The interviews were characterized by an intimacy and an intensity that belied their structure and standardization. Several of the interviews, in fact, grew quite poignant as people confessed what they perceived to be their personal failings and conflicts. Despite this potential for pain, the interviews were apparently worthwhile for them as well as for me. Several sent me letters shortly afterward. The following excerpt is fairly typical: "I enjoyed the interview and talking with you about myself in terms of workaholism. While I don't like to think of myself in those terms, maybe I learned some new things."

In the course of conducting the interviews, compiling the questionnaire responses, and writing this book, there was no question that I fit right in with the rest of the workaholics. My typist tried to keep up with me and usually succeeded. I would give her material at 7:30 Sunday night only to get it back at 7:30 Monday morning. I wondered when—and if—she slept, and the solicitude was reciprocal. She asked me whether I went out enough.

Indeed, I broke more than one date because I couldn't pull myself away from my desk. Once, however, I made a special attempt to keep a Saturday night dinner date. I got up at 6 A.M. and stayed at my desk until 6 P.M. Glancing at the clock, I called my friend and asked him if he would come over at 7:00 instead of 6:30, as we'd arranged in advance. After all, I had not yet even dressed that day, let alone made dinner. Then, at 6:30, I called him again. Would he, I pleaded, please stop at the deli on his way over and buy something for us to eat?

Contents

A Day in the Life

My day starts at about 4:15 in the morning when I wake up, and I leave the house by about 4:45 or 5:00. I'm in the office at 5:30, 5:35 at the latest.

I have coffee all morning and lunch at about 12:00. I generally try to keep it down to an hour or an hour and a half if it's a business lunch. If it's possible, I'll just grab a sandwich in the office.

I keep two meetings going on at once most of the time. I have a conference room attached to this office. I keep one meeting going on in there and generally will have a second meeting started in here, and my next meeting waiting in there. So I just go from one to the other.

I'll generally have a business appointment for dinner at around 10:00 that'll last about an hour and a half and then [I'll] go home. If I don't have a dinner appointment, I leave the office between 10:00 and 11:00.

I only sleep three and a half to four hours a night; I start to get tired if I cut it below three.

Frank S. Berger, former president of
The House of Seagram

1
Workaholism:
What It Is

No ethic is as ethical as the work ethic.
—John Kenneth Galbraith

All around us, signs, symptoms, and signals seem to suggest that the almighty, all-American work ethic is eroding. Factory workers opt for time off instead of overtime. Students seem to favor self-worth over net worth; they aim, they say, for fun, family life, and $30,000 a year. They won't slave away for $60,000, as dear old dad may have done. Upwardly mobile executives are refusing to move when their companies ask them to relocate. And social scientists persistently portray a workforce that suffers from the white collar woes as well as the blue collar blues.

Employers have adjusted. Mandatory transfers have been removed from many career paths. Menial jobs have been enriched and enlarged almost beyond recognition. Experiments with time—from four-day workweeks to "flextime"—have rearranged and, in some cases, reduced the total time spent working. Even President Carter, in an impassioned speech to his staff soon after taking office, expressed opposition to the overwork characteristic of earlier administrations. He said, in part, "All of you will be more valuable to me and the country with rest and a stable home life."

In spite of President Carter's well-publicized wishes to the contrary, his aides and associates still work well into the night. One White House cleaning woman apparently complained that David Rubinstein, a deputy to presidential advisor Stuart Eizenstat, doesn't leave his office long enough for her to dust it. Former H.E.W. secretary Joseph Califano's appetite for work cost taxpayers plenty: He reportedly had to hire a second shift of secretaries and installed a separate air-conditioning system for those times when the main unit is shut off. And the president himself isn't practicing what he once preached: His eighteen-hour day led one wag to christen him "The Bionic Grind."

Elsewhere in Washington the story is the same. In *The Powers That Be,* David Halberstam described Robert Woodward, *The Washington Post* reporter of Watergate fame, as

> a totally compulsive person, a classic workaholic, wildly ambitious, utterly obsessed by his work and his career. . . . His work habits were terrifying. Even before Watergate the regular work hours of the *Post* were not enough for him. He had once come in very late at night on his own, bored with

his life, and had gone out, in lieu of anything else
to do, to interview construction workers building
the new subway system in Washington, the only
available interviewees at that hour.

When Robert Redford was preparing to portray
Robert Woodward in the movie *All the President's
Men,* he told *Rolling Stone* just how hard Washing-
tonians work. "Washington," he concluded, "is a re-
ceptacle for workaholics."

He may be right. Dr. John Meeks of The
Psychiatric Institute of Washington finds that in our
nation's capital, workaholism "is accepted as normal. If you look at people in government by any ra-
tional standards, they're all workaholics. It's routine
to work sixty- to seventy-hour weeks. . . . It seems to
be as American as apple pie."

Attorney Harvey L. Pitt, for instance, went from
law school to the Securities and Exchange Commis-
sion and then to the prestigious law firm of Fried,
Frank, Harris, Shriver & Kampelmen, where he
routinely works twelve to fifteen hours a day during
the week. He cuts down to only nine or ten a day on
weekends. Such work habits are so well entrenched
in our country's capital that *Business Week* advised
Washington-bound executives to remember "that the
busiest officials often work on Saturday and sometimes even on Sunday, [so] a weekend appointment
is something to suggest."

Lest one suspect that these workers are isolated,
dedicated individuals who are merely responding to
the demands of duty, ample evidence exists to
suggest that such work patterns are self-imposed. A

former "Nader's Raider" continued to work twelve
hours a day, seven days a week, long after leaving
consumer advocate Ralph Nader's staff. She told a
reporter that it wasn't just the job that warranted
working that hard. *She* was the one who required
that kind of workload.

Although Washington seems to attract an un-
usually large number of workaholics, New York City
also fosters them. *New York Times* music critic
Harold C. Schonberg feels that "New York really is
faster than the rest of the world. If you live in New
York and expect to get anywhere, you have to hop to
it. You move faster, talk faster, work faster."

Even New York City's 1977 blackout couldn't
keep workaholics at home. Several hundreds of
people went to work despite the knowledge that
buildings would be locked and businesses closed. I
found them pacing impatiently outside their offices,
demanding to be allowed to enter, even if reaching
their desks would require climbing thirty flights of
stairs. Others went about their business on the street.
One vice president of Booz, Allen & Hamilton, a
leading management consulting firm, sat on the
steps outside 245 Park Avenue working with a
hand-held calculator. His only concern was that the
calculator's batteries might require recharging before
electricity was restored. Quite a few others con-
ducted impromptu conferences while perched on
their briefcases all along the sidewalks or, as a con-
cession to the day's 100° F heat, inside air-
conditioned cars. One such conferring pair, seated at
a Park Avenue plaza, concluded, "We probably got

more done out here." When I asked a senior Pan Am executive why he bothered commuting at all or why he didn't just go home, he told me, "I have too much to do to stay home."

Workaholism isn't just peculiar to the East Coast. At the other side of the country, even seemingly laid-back Californians may be closet workaholics. As a West Coast woman reported, "In California we try to act casual as if we've been playing tennis all day, but in reality, I work as hard here as I did in New York—but pretend not to."

Who are all of these people and why are they working so hard? They're work junkies—workaholics—and they are addicted to their jobs. They love their work. They *live* their work. And most of them find it very difficult to ever leave their work, even in extreme circumstances. One elderly attorney toiled away while his office building burned down around him. He ignored the warnings, sirens, and screams until he was finally forcibly ejected by firefighters. A pregnant publicist I know was enjoying the rare luxury of a leisurely lunch when she felt her first labor pains. She rushed from the restaurant to her obstetrician's office. When he assured her that delivery was still hours away, she went back to work.

So, despite the dire warnings that opened this chapter, the work ethic is not only alive and well, but in certain circles it is flourishing. As psychologist Robert L. Kahn suggests, "There's no viable alternative to work, no other activity that uses energy, demands attention, provides regular social interaction

around some visible outcome, and does so in a socially approved way."[1]

As retirees rapidly come to realize, a job provides a lot more than just a paycheck. Jobs structure
people's time. They permit regular interpersonal interaction and provide a sense of identity, self-esteem,
and self-respect. But for all these positive effects at-
tributed to working, alienated workers have received
far more of scholars' attention than have their highly
absorbed counterparts, the workaholics.

The popular press has paid some attention to
work addicts. It's an unusual business magazine that
doesn't mention the word at least once per issue.
One career guide advises job applicants to answer
the inevitable question "What are your weaknesses?"
with a quality that is apt to be attractive to a prospective employer. It tells readers to say, "I'm
such a workaholic that I tend to get completely
caught up in my work." And a women's magazine
told its readers to end a summer or vacation romance
by warning men about being a workaholic back at
home.

But there is scant scientific research on workaholics. My own master's thesis and doctoral dissertation were the first systematic studies of the phenomenon. My best estimate suggests that workaholics comprise no more than 5 percent of the adult
population. They probably make up a slightly higher
percentage of the workforce, since workaholics are
the least likely to be unemployed. Somehow, it
seems, workaholics have overcome or averted the

difficulties and dissatisfactions that plague today's workers. Perhaps, once workaholism is better
understood, it will be possible to use the experience
of the work addict to enrich and enhance the working lives of others. But first we need to dispel some of
the negative attitudes we have about workaholics.

Most descriptions of the phenomenon do not
define workaholism as much as they denigrate and
deride workaholics. Lotte Bailyn of M.I.T. described
the workaholic as the "victim of a newly recognized
social disease presumably responsible for the disin-
tegration of the family, [and] for severe distortion of
full personal development."[2] Likewise, a respected
New York Times writer, Charlotte Curtis, portrayed the workaholic as someone who was "anxious, guilt-ridden, insecure, or self righteous about
. . . work. . . . a slave to a set schedule, merciless
in his demands upon himself for peak performance
. . . compulsively overcommitted."

The word "workaholism" owes its origin, as
well as its negative overtones, to "alcoholism." What
distinguishes workaholism from other addictions is
that workaholism is sometimes considered a virtue,
while others, such as alcoholism, or drug addiction,
are invariably considered vices.

Yet workaholics are usually portrayed as a miserable lot. This bias stems from the ways we learn
about them. The clergy hears their confessions;
physicians and therapists, their complaints; and
judges, their divorces. The few articles about workaholics that have appeared in scientific journals typ-

ically emphasize the psychosocial problems of specific patients. The workaholics that I interviewed
had few such problems.

Another major bias against workaholics are the
beliefs of nonworkaholics. People who work to live
cannot understand those who live to work and love
it. They watch in amazement and wonder about
those who delight in what they do. Workaholics' un-
orthodox attitude—that their work is so much fun
they'd probably do it for free—causes nonworkaholics
to question their own situation. The latter group begins to worry "What's wrong with my job?" or,
worse, "What's wrong with me?" To resolve these
feelings, nonworkaholics resort to denouncing
workaholics rather than running down themselves.
They say, "Sure, workaholics are successful at work,
but aren't they really ruining the rest of their lives?"
This logic is akin to that of "Lucky in cards, unlucky
in love" and equally untrue. Satisfaction with work
and with life are more apt to be intertwined than
mutually exclusive.

Workaholism is almost exclusively American,
but it is also un-American. You are *supposed* to lead
lives that are well-rounded, balanced, and more
"normal" than those of workaholics. Sure, you
should go to work weekdays, but you better not
spend evenings and weekends at work, as well.
Those times should be spent with the family or playing ball or seeing friends or gardening. Have you
ever heard of a beauty pageant contestant who
couldn't list at least half a dozen hobbies, from basket
weaving to opera singing? In contrast, when faced

with an employment application, a workaholic might have to leave that item blank. Workaholics are more willing to settle for excellence in one endeavor and to admit that they are inept and uninterested in anything else. As playwright Neil Simon said (italics mine), "I wish I *could* do other things well besides write, . . . play an instrument, learn other languages, cook, ski. My greatest sense of accomplishment is that I didn't waste time *trying* to learn those things."

Nor is it American to like your job that much, and those who do are suspect. To look forward to Monday instead of Friday is regarded as strange and even abnormal. Production workers attach posters to their machines that say "Hang in there; Friday's coming." In the executive suites such signs are understandably absent, but sentiments like "Thank God it's Friday" are frequently heard.

As a result, workaholics are often openly maligned. A top health insurance organization placed a full-page magazine ad warning of the alleged health hazards and related costs of working too hard. The photo featured an angry-looking man with a cigarette dangling from his lips and butts spilling out of an overflowing ashtray; his tie loosened, his collar undone, his shirt straining at his paunch, a styrofoam coffee cup in one hand and several others strewn about an incredibly cluttered desk. The headline read, "He's working twelve hours a day to increase the cost of health care." The copy continued, "In the Horatio Alger story the hero works day and night to get ahead and everybody looks up to him

with admiration. Now, millions of Americans are following this example. . . . we're not asking you to
stop working. Just try not to overdo it. And when you
see someone who thinks he's Horatio Alger, don't
think of him as a hero. Think of him as a villain."

Most workaholics won't admit that's what they
are because the word has such negative connota-
tions. In fact, so many of the people I interviewed
objected to the word that I frequently substituted
other phrases ("the role of work in the lives of successful hard workers") when talking to them.
Everyone I interviewed acknowledged that they had
been accused of being a workaholic. And almost all
admitted that my characteristics of workaholism
came a little too close for comfort. As television an-
chorwoman Jessica Savitch wrote me, "I do not like
the label since it conjures up a negative addiction
such as alcoholic. But the qualities you ascribe
to a workaholic are qualities I seek and admire in
others."

Not everyone, however, dismisses workaholics
as dismal or dangerous. When a young mathemati-
cian heard I was writing a book about workaholics,
he eagerly asked me, "Does your book tell how to
become one?" And, indeed, in certain governmen-
tal, professional, and academic circles, workaholism
has managed to develop considerable cachet. In, say,
Washington, D.C., New York City, or Cambridge,
Massachusetts, you can hear quite a few people
claim to be workaholics. I, for one, doubt that too
many of them really are simply because they brag

about it. Real workaholics will doubt, demur, or deny outright that that's what they are.

Then, too, workaholics do not necessarily recognize or realize just how hard they do work. But they don't mind working hard. While the masses may moan and grumble about having to work hard, workaholics enjoy and exult in it. In fact, Dr. John Rhoads, a psychiatrist on the faculty of Duke University, maintains that it is almost axiomatic that those who complain of being overworked are not.[3] For example, Dick Vermeil, head coach of Philadelphia's pro football team, the Eagles, and a man who is invariably called a workaholic, told me, "I don't actually know what the word means, but I am tired of its being used in describing my personality. I do what I'm doing because I enjoy it very much and really don't consider it hard work."

While workaholics do work hard, not all hard workers are workaholics. I will use the word workaholic to describe those whose desire to work long and hard is intrinsic and whose work habits almost always exceed the prescriptions of the job they do and the expectations of the people with whom or for whom they work. But the first characteristic is the real determinant. What truly distinguishes workaholics from other hard workers is that the others work only to please a boss, earn a promotion, or meet a deadline. Moonlighters, for example, may work sixteen hours a day merely to make ends meet, but most of them stop working multiple shifts as soon as their financial circumstances permit. Accountants, too, may sometimes seem to work non-stop, but most slow down markedly after April 15th. For workaholics, on the other hand, the workload seldom lightens, for they don't *want* to work less. As Senator William Proxmire has found, "The less I work, the less I enjoy it."

Time spent working would be an appealing index of workaholism, but it would also be a misleading measure. Although workaholics may work from 5 A.M. to 9 P.M. instead of the more usual 9 A.M. to 5 P.M., the hours they work are not the *sine qua non* of workaholism. It is in fact preferable to view workaholism as an approach or an attitude toward working than as an amount of time at work. Workaholics will continue to think about work when they're not working—even at moments that are, well, inappropriate. One energy specialist recalls dreaming about Con Ed and seeing barrels of oil in her sleep. One research and development director mentally designs new studies while making love to his wife.

But numbers and totals do count: Workaholics are given to counting their work hours and especially their achievements. Dr. Denton Cooley, the founder and chief surgeon of the Texas Heart Institute of Houston, enclosed a six-page vitae and a two-page biography with his finished questionnaire, which was handwritten in the illegible scrawl for which physicians are famous. The vitae listed a string of international honors; the biography, his achievements: By 1978, Cooley had performed over 30,000 open heart operations, more than any other

surgeon in the world. He and his staff perform 25 to
30 such operations a day. An aide explains:

> I don't think you'll talk to anyone who likes to op-
> erate more than Cooley. People like him don't go
> into medicine for mankind. They do it because they
> like it. I mean he could relax, he doesn't need the
> money. His dad was a successful dentist who in-
> vested very wisely in Houston real estate. And Den-
> ton's surgical fees are more than one million dol-
> lars a year. But he just wouldn't be happy if he
> couldn't operate every day. Hell, I've seen him call
> in from a morning meeting in New York to set up
> an afternoon surgery schedule. The guy is hooked.[4]

Dr. Cooley defended his dedication far more simply.
He works as he does, he said, "because I enjoy it."

Workaholism is not restricted to hospital corri-
dors, Congressional offices, or elegant executive suites.
While we sneer at it in corporate executives, workaholism is something we've come to accept—and
even admire—in artists, and it is what we expect
of our personal physicians. It is also part and par-
cel of our image of most scientists, such as Edison
and Einstein. As Wilfred J. Corrigan, former chairman of Fairchild Camera and Instrument Corporation told *Business Week,* "A lot of people in this
industry are totally involved with their work.
Everyone sees this as appropriate for an artist paint-
ing the Sistine chapel or an author writing a novel.
But in science and technology, there are times when
you just don't want to go home."

Although I interviewed far more white collar
than blue collar workers, I found that workaholics

exist in every occupation, from managers and doctors to secretaries and assembly line workers. One
man had a combined M.D.–Ph.D.; another had only a
high school diploma. A friend once described her
apartment building's janitor as a workaholic. "I feel
very fortunate," she said, "to have a super who's a
compulsive worker. He won't even stop and talk.
Occasionally, he'll have a conversation with someone while he's sweeping the sidewalk."

Nor is workaholism restricted to just one sex.
While women have been almost completely overlooked in the little that has been written about workaholism, there have always been women workaholics. If housework, for instance, were rightfully
regarded as work, generations of compulsive cleaners could be considered workaholics. And so would
the tireless organizers of charity events. Today, women's workaholism is merely more apparent, since
more and more women work outside their homes.

Dr. Helen De Rosis, associate clinical professor
of psychiatry at New York University School of
Medicine and the author of several books about
women, cautions against confusing women workaholics with the so-called Superwomen. A Superwoman tries to be Supermom and Superwife as well
as Superworker. Superwoman, according to syndicated columnist Ellen Goodman, is not only a Wonder Woman at work but an elegant dresser and an
excellent cook as well. Her kids do not subsist on
cold cereal: Superwoman gets up at the crack of
dawn to make them a hot, nutritious, and nitrite-free
breakfast. Her husband has a delicious dinner every

night: She not only has time to get the groceries, but to whip up gourmet delights, courtesy of Julia Child and Cuisinart. Her relationship with her children is characterized, of course, by the *quality*—not by the quantity—of the time she spends with them. Similarly, her marriage can only be called a meaningful relationship. She and her husband are not only each other's best friend but also ecstatic lovers, because Superwoman is never too tired at night. Instead, she is, in the words of Ellen Goodman, "multiorgasmic until midnight."[5]

According to Dr. De Rosis, whose books include *Women and Anxiety*, Superwomen and workaholics share a basic similarity: Both use their work as a defense against anxiety. While workaholics appear to enjoy their work, Dr. De Rosis explains that the enjoyment they experience is distinct from the pleasure felt by women who are able to shift their priorities for different occasions. "The workaholic can't do this. She can't say, 'Today I'll stay home because my child is sick.' She can't make that decision."

Nor should women workaholics be mistaken for women who must do double time to make up for sex-related obstacles in their careers. When Monica Bauer joined Xerox in 1966, she found that she "really did have to put in more time than my male associates just to get the information." Back then, Bauer was excluded from the "old boy network" and other informal channels of communication and had no "new girl network" to turn to. The times have changed, but Bauer's drive shows no decline. She continues to put in long days at Xerox, where she is now manager of low volume products and pricing, and recently completed an M.B.A. at the University of Rochester while working full-time.

So, despite the fact that workaholics come from all classes, sexes, and occupations, they all share one over-riding passion: work. After interviewing more than one hundred work addicts over several years, I have some good news and some bad news. The good news is that as a group, workaholics are surprisingly happy. They are doing exactly what they love—work—and they can't seem to get enough of it. If the circumstances are right—that is, if their jobs fit and their families are accommodating—then workaholics can be astonishingly productive. But here's the bad news: The people who work with and live with workaholics often suffer. Adjusting to the frenetic schedule of a workaholic is not easy and only rarely rewarding. At work these addicts are often demanding and sometimes not very effective. At home, well, you'll seldom find a workaholic at home. The tensions implicit in this rather unbalanced life-style cause very real dilemmas for those involved, and a good part of this book is about those problems.

QUIZ: ARE YOU A WORKAHOLIC?

Who are these work addicts and what makes them tick? What's wrong with being a workaholic, and more importantly, what's right about it? In my research I have found that, despite disparate circumstances, most workaholics share a common set of characteristics, which I will discuss in the next chapter. In order to identify workaholics I've developed a quiz based on these characteristics. If you've ever wondered whether you're a workaholic—or if you think you might be working or living with one—take this test and see.

	YES	NO

1. *Do you get up early, no matter how late you go to bed?*
   As one management consultant confessed, "I'd get home and work until [about] 2 A.M., and then get up at 5 A.M. and think, 'Gee, aren't I terrific!' "

2. *If you are eating lunch alone, do you read or work while you eat?*
   Robert Moses, New York's long-time Parks Commissioner, reportedly considered lunches a bore and a bother because he couldn't bear to interrupt work. He used a large table as a desk so lunch could be served right there.

3. *Do you make daily lists of thing to do?*
   Ever-present appointment books and cluttered calendars are a hallmark of workaholics. Indeed, their main way of wasting time, admits Dr. Elizabeth Whelan, a Harvard University epidemiologist, may be looking for lost lists!

4. *Do you find it difficult to "do nothing"?*

It was claimed that David Mahoney,
the handsome, hard-working chairman
of Norton Simon, Inc., abandoned
transcendental meditation because he
found it impossible to sit still for
twenty minutes.   YES   NO

5. *Are you energetic and competitive?*   ☐   ☐
   President Johnson once asked Doris
   Kearns, then a White House Fellow, if
   she were energetic. Kearns replied, "I
   hear you need only five hours of sleep,
   but I need only four so it stands to
   reason that I've got even more energy
   than you."[6]

6. *Do you work on weekends and holi-
   days?*   ☐   ☐
   In *Working*, author Studs Terkel related that the president of a Chicago
   radio station confessed that he regu-
   larly works in his home on weekends.
   But, he added, "when I do this on holidays, like Christmas, New Year's, and
   Thanksgiving, I have to sneak a bit so
   the family doesn't know what I'm doing."

7. *Can you work anytime and anywhere?* ☐   ☐
   Two associates at Cravath, Swaine and
   Moore, one of Manhattan's most prestigious law firms, were said to have
   bet about who could bill the most
   hours in a day. One worked around

the clock, billed twenty-four, and felt
assured of victory. His competitor,
however, having flown to California in
the course of the day and worked on
the plane, was able to bill twenty-
seven.

8. *Do you find vacations "hard to take"?* YES ☐ NO ☐
George Lois, the art director who
heads Lois Pitts Gershon, an advertising agency, had to think a while when
I asked him when he had taken his
last vacation. Finally, he recalled
when it was: 1964—almost fourteen
years before!

9. *Do you dread retirement?* ☐ ☐
After retiring from the ad agency
where she had created such classic
slogans as Clairol's "Does she . . . or
doesn't she?" Shirley Polykoff started
her own advertising agency. As president of Shirley Polykoff Advertising in
New York she still—some six years
later—has no plans to slow up or step
down. She says, "I'm doing more now
than I've ever done. I don't know how
you retire if you're still healthy and
exuberant about living. They'll have to
carry me out in a box!"

10. *Do you really enjoy your work?* ☐ ☐
As Joyce Carol Oates, the Canadian
novelist, once told *The New York*

Times, "I am not conscious of working
especially hard, or of 'working' at
all. . . . Writing and teaching have
always been, for me, so richly rewarding that I do not think of them as work
in the usual sense of the word."

If you answered "Yes" to eight or more questions,
you, too, may be a workaholic.

2
Workaholics:
Who They Are and What They're Like

To rest is to rust.
—Lester Lanin

When I interviewed Dr. Stuart Berger, who is now an associate professor of psychiatry at Harvard, he was 25 and wrapping up his final days at New York City's Bellevue Hospital. A tall, good-looking man with dark, curly hair, Berger was wearing jeans and Adidas, almost as much a part of the uniform of a young doctor as the beeper attached to his belt. We met in his small apartment, which was dominated by both its imposing view of the New York skyline and a large, well-stocked wine rack. The interview was interrupted by incessant phone calls, for which Berger apologized, explaining, "My life has been a bit busy."

And indeed it had. Besides seeing private patients, teaching psychiatry and law, directing an institute for the study of law and medicine, consulting

for a drug-free therapeutic community, seeing clinic
patients, supervising medical students and junior
residents, and writing a book, Berger had been flying
around the country to lecture and appear on television talk shows.

"My average week is about 100 hours long and
very fast-paced. I get up about 6 A.M., shower, and
have coffee; start reading journals at 6:30; see my
first patients at 8:00; teach; never eat lunch—I just
have garbage food all day. Three-quarters of the time
I have a work-related dinner, and it's not uncommon
on private days to see patients until 8:00, 8:30 at
night. Of course, there's something very important
to say about this horrendous-sounding schedule: I
adore it!"

What makes him go and what keeps him going?
"Give me a good goal. Give me something I can get
excited about, that I can fantasize about, that I can
live. I don't need any thank yous. I don't need any
appreciation. I just need something I can get excited
about. . . . I absolutely crave psychiatry and love
developing better systems for providing patient care.
And these are things I can work on for months at a
time at this pace. The goals are never accomplish-
able. There are always going to be more social problems. There'll never be an end. No matter how much
I accomplish, it'll always be trivial compared to
what's left to be done."

When asked what he does when he's not working, he paused and was hard-pressed to come up
with anything. "What kinds of things do I like? I

have to think of them. I've given up collecting coins and I'd always been a great reader before I went to college." Having just bought a summer home, he was planning to spend time there. "I'm taking three-day weekends. People who know me don't believe it. I'll read the books that have been piling up for seven years, sail, lose some weight, jog, and make myself healthy before I go into hibernation again."

But even as he spoke, Berger began to doubt his words. Smiling sheepishly, he said, "Call me up at the end of the summer and I'll tell you if I did it."

If Berger has taken the quiz at the end of the last chapter, he probably would have scored 100 percent. He has most of the earmarks of the workaholic: He is intense and driven, he doesn't sleep much, he works almost all of his waking hours, and vacations and time off remain firmly in the realm of fantasy. Berger's workaholic tendencies seem to fit well with his job and with his single, busy life-style. He is what I call a fulfilled workaholic, one who gets great enjoyment from his work and who has successfully shaped the rest of his life around his central passion.

Others, especially those with families, have more difficulty accomplishing such a feat. Alex Loukides (a pseudonym) is a typical example. Brought up in a lower class Greek community in Connecticut, Loukides graduated from college and served in the Marines before he joined the Manhattan firm where he still works. Loukides is 41, his wife is a few years younger, and their two children are 12 and 14. Loukides is now a senior partner in the

firm. Whereas most of his colleagues commute from
lush suburbs, he still lives in the town where he
grew up, despite his substantial six-figure income.

We met in his office at 7:30 one morning.
Loukides was trim, tailored, immaculately attired,
and awfully alert despite having already been at
work for an hour. He served me a terrible cup of cold
instant coffee. It was cold because he couldn't bear to
wait for the water to boil. It was instant because his
secretary wouldn't arrive for at least another hour.

His present position is, he says, more "unpredictable" and therefore more "exhilarating" than
any of the many he has held since his trainee days.
Still, he says, "I feel the same getting off the elevator
as I did twenty years ago. There's no sense of power
or anything like that." He cites his success in business as his main source of satisfaction, explaining, "I
don't think you can separate yourself from what you
do. I don't think your concept of yourself can be
separated from what you do."

Loukides is frequently in his Manhattan office
six days a week. He arrives home around 8 P.M. His
travel schedule is less time-consuming than it could
be, however, for when he travels, he resorts to turnaround trips: "I've been to Paris thirteen times for a
total of twelve days."

Nor are vacations a temptation. "Vacations bore
me. I don't really enjoy them. . . . In the past few
years, I've made a real effort to take them. We bought
a house by the shore. This was an effort on my part to
force me to spend time with my family."

Not surprisingly, he feels guilty about "not having been as good a husband and a father as I'd like to be. . . . I don't think the kids resent my working [hard]. . . . I think my wife does . . . . she's a housewife and she's going through the same thing every other woman's going through. 'Should I go back to school? Should I get a job?' I don't try to discourage her, but I find it kind of threatening, too. It's sort of comfortable for me to have her in the house."

Regarding his own future plans, Loukides is both adamant and uncertain. "I won't retire. I'll have a second career. . . . how much longer can I stay here? I'll either be blocking someone, or I'll be running the show. And you can't do that for more than five years, so I'll have to have a second career. But, I mean, just retiring . . . I don't think it's necessary, and I don't think it's healthy."

When I asked him if he was a workaholic, Loukides said, "I don't know. If you asked my wife, she would say 'Definitely.' And probably a lot of other people would, too. . . . If being a workaholic means you're dependent on work and you have to have work in order to function, well, I think that's true for everybody."

Loukides seemed vaguely aware of some rumblings both in the office (his "unpredictable" position) and at home. Yet he either doesn't see clearly or chooses not to accept that some of these problems could be tied to his addiction for work.

Both Loukides and Berger share six basic characteristics that set all workaholics apart. These "traits" indicate that workaholism is considerably

more paradoxical than the stereotype would lead us
to believe. Still, my research shows that these characteristics are common to each and every workaholic
that I interviewed. Let's take a look at them.

*Workaholics are intense, energetic, competitive,
and driven.* The intensity of a workaholic is inspiring. Eileen Ford, founder and head of the New York
modeling agency, skips much of the weekend social
scene. "It's not the good life that interests me so
much as the good job." She explains that she spends
her weekends working. "I lock myself in my bedroom on Saturday and Sunday with shades drawn
and work until I accomplish what I wish to accomplish."

Part of the ability to work so hard, finds Mrs.
Ford, comes from working at what one enjoys. "If I'm
working, that's just what I am doing, nothing else.
I'm not thinking about what else I would like to do,
only what I'm doing. My mind doesn't wander. I am
capable of tremendous concentration. I am never
tired."

Workaholics also have an overwhelming zest for
life. They are people who wake up and can't wait to
get going. A banker explained, "I have a tremendous
amount of energy. . . . my father says Con Ed
should have plugged into me during the energy
crisis." Already energetic, workaholics are energized
rather than enervated by their work—their energy
paradoxically expands as it is expended. This relationship between energy and work is somewhat cir-
cular. As an advertising executive explained, "My

energy contributes to my job and my job contributes to my energy."

Workaholics compete fiercely with others. However, the most stringent standards are internal and the strongest competition is with themselves. As one man explained, "I live on ten-year goals. . . . I set my own goals, make my own challenges, and compete with myself." They live life as a game—better yet, a race—to be won for fear that others will gain on them unless they keep getting ahead. One workaholic delighted in getting to work hours before anyone else because, "by 9:00 I had done a day's work. . . . I was already a day ahead of everybody."

Not surprisingly, the number one topic for comparison in this competition is hours of work. A young physician explained that the main obsession among his medical school classmates, the residents who supervised them in hospital wards, and the physicians who taught them the courses wasn't money, sex, or knowledge, but how hard they worked. Five-minute lunches never left much time for conversation, but this topic was always discussed.

Workaholics are driven. While waiting for the critical and commercial success that will permit him to move from Manhattan and television to Hollywood and the movies, a young screenwriter holds a full-time job as a staff writer for a mundane trade magazine. He considers himself a workaholic "because I totally define myself in terms of my work. . . . I'm so used to its directing my life. It's directing me. I'm not directing it. . . . But it's gone too far. I can't not do it. I get physically sick if I don't do something on a script each day. . . ."

His drive is not derived from a sense of self-discipline. Rather, his seeming self-discipline stems from his drive. "Writing gives me discipline. You have to be home at a certain time to write." He is not one to do nothing. "Intellectually, I realize there's a value to rest, [to] 'hanging out,' 'bumming around,' but emotionally, I can't."

Workaholics have strong self-doubts. Although they appear assured to the point of arrogance, they secretly suspect that they are inadequate. No matter how undeserved and/or suppressed these suspicions are, they still inspire insecurities. Working hard can be a way of concealing or compensating for such suspected shortcomings.

Shelly Gross is a producer, novelist, and co-founder of Music Fair Enterprises, Inc., an organization that produces shows and concerts throughout the United States and Canada. Gross' workweek typically includes commuting between suburban Philadelphia, where he lives and works, and Manhattan, where partner Lee Guber lives and works; catching new acts; and throwing cast suppers in each city. His strategy, like that of most workaholics, is to organize his time. "I try my best compulsively not to waste time." Gross feels uneasy when forced to waste time, so he makes sure that he's seldom put in that position: He fills his time with surf fishing and writing; he's finished five novels so far. What makes

Shelly run? "Deep down inside, there's the feeling that I'm trading sweat for talent."

This concern is not uncommon. One man felt he wasn't quite the intellectual equal of his peers, despite his Harvard degrees. Therefore, he thought the only way to keep up would be by doing more. Others maintain that their work isn't just the thing they're best at, but the only thing they're even good at. Barbara Walters, for instance, squelches claims that she is an all-around Wonder Woman with an appealing combination of honesty and modesty. She told *Vogue* magazine, "I flunked gym, flunked home economics. I am not visual and can't draw. But I'm compulsive. Whatever it is, I must do it today. And must do it over until it's right."

Workaholics prefer labor to leisure. With respect to weekends and vacations, the ways of workaholics once again appear to be at odds with those of the rest of society. Either because of position or personality, they have blended or reversed the customary roles, preferring labor to leisure. What they do for a living has evolved into an endlessly fascinating endeavor. They have no use for and little need of free time. They find inactivity intolerable and pressure preferable. Workaholics never say "Thank God it's Friday" for they prefer weekdays to weekends. Mondays, in fact, offer welcome relief from the "Sunday neurosis," a syndrome of anxiety and depression stimulated by a weekend's tranquility.

Workaholics can—and do—work anytime and anywhere. They are heedless of holidays, slow sea-

sons, and weekends. Many maintain that they save
time this way. Explains Senator William Proxmire "I
find that by working on weekends or evenings or
times when the phone is not ringing and others are
not present, it is possible to accomplish a lot in a
short time." Nor are they likely to turn off after
hours. As a securities analyst said, "I'm forever
thinking about new companies and new industries
and, to a degree, this puts me in my office twenty-
four hours a day."

As a result, their homes often become but branch
offices of their businesses and both airplanes and
commuter trains are pressed into service as substitute offices. Mary Wells Lawrence, who heads Wells,
Rich, Greene, a New York ad agency, was once asked
by a reporter when she stops, slows down, turns off,
tunes out. She replied, "Never. I am either digesting
new material or looking for new solutions to a
client's problem. When I'm on a plane, I don't waste
a minute. I cover all the magazines—I demolish
them. I see a picture of a yacht we could photograph,
read about a restaurant to take clients to or a new
take-out place for chili because there's a client who
likes chili."[1]

Workaholics make the most of their time. Their
attitude toward time and its use is their most telling
trait: The quest to conquer time is constant. They
glance at their watches continually, as though cal-
culating how to fit the most work into the least
amount of time. Saving time becomes a goal in itself
as they put to good use the spare seconds others
seem not to notice. As Stanley Marcus, the depart-

ment store magnate, stated in Minding the Store,
"Time is a precious possession and I attempt to make
the most of it by not wasting it, for it is irreplaceable.
One of the ways I cover so much ground is by using
time judiciously. . . . we all have time to do everything we want to do if we organize our time
properly."

For workaholics, "killing time" would seem tantamount to commiting suicide. As in Max Weber's
explanation of the tenets of the Protestant ethic,
"Waste of time is thus the first and in principle dead-
liest of sins." So they sleep six hours a night (at
most) and get up and get going early. Their meals are
typically functional (breakfast business meetings) or
fast (lunch at the desk). They use lists, appointment
books, and gadgets—the dictating devices, lighted
pens for darkened rooms, and even car telephones
that enable them to work wherever they are—to master every minute. Indeed, workaholics are so conscious of and compulsive about using every minute
that they struggle to save seconds. They are the ones
who continually punch the elevator button and then
take the stairs because they don't want to wait. They
rush through the day and into the night. As one harried woman reported, "I feel I even have to sleep
fast."

They fill their Daytimers months in advance.
And as Mary Wells Lawrence told Vogue, "I run my
life the way a lot of people run their businesses; I
have to. I don't literally draw charts and graphs, but
it's how I think. Everything is written down, planned
in advance. I plan the year, I plan the month, I plan

the week, I plan the day." Workaholics will win
whenever being booked up becomes something of a
status game. And a game it is. Jack Lenor Larsen, the
New York fabric designer, cheerfully concedes that
"to do ten things in one day would be too much, but
to try for fifteen becomes an interesting game."

*Workaholics blur the distinctions between busi-
ness and pleasure.* Louis L'Amour, the prolific
novelist, maintains that "the things I would do for
fun are the things necessary to my work anyway. My
work is also my hobby. I am happiest when working." One workaholic told me, "I don't think of work
as any different from play. I mean, I do enjoy it—I'd
rather do that than anything else. I'd rather do that
than play—at anything else. I don't know why one
has to draw the distinction."

As a result, the professional and personal lives
of these work addicts become intertwined. "Some of
my best friends are people I've met over a conference
table . . . and some of my clients are people I've met
at parties," explained Laurel Cutler, senior vice-
president for marketing planning at Leber Katz
Partners in New York.

Although each and every workaholic exhibits
these characteristics, workaholics do differ from one
another. The variation involves their attitude toward
nonwork activities. Some workaholics, as the stereotype suggests, eschew these entirely. Others incorporate them into their work in one of several ways.

My research revealed four distinct types of
workaholics.

 The Dedicated Workaholic. The first type of workaholic is single-minded and one-dimensional. These people fit the stereotype to a "T." They don't expand "job descriptions" to include their other interests because they simply have no other interests. They often seem humorless and brusque—and they are. As one executive recruiter confessed, "I'm so single-minded. I have to work very hard at not working twenty-four hours a day." Lew Wasserman, chairman of M.C.A., Inc., the entertainment conglomerate, has no hobbies. According to *Fortune,* "he admits with seeming pride that he has never played a set of tennis or round of golf, and that in his forty-year career with M.C.A. he has taken but a single vacation." And Leda Sanford, a magazine editor, reportedly hates sports, spurns theatre and ballet, and is never without her briefcase.

Similarly, Revlon's Charles Revson was said to be particularly single-minded and exclusively devoted to his business. One of his associates once wished to interrupt a meeting momentarily to glance out the window as the Pope's motorcade passed by on Fifth Avenue. Revson was said to be indignant and totally uninterested in the historic procession below. The Vatican, after all, was not a prime purchaser of nail polish and lipstick.

The Integrated Workaholic. For the second type of workaholics, work is also "everything," but their work includes outside interests as well. By virtue of their job's purpose or their own personalities, they incorporate outside activities into the job itself. The president of one management consulting firm claimed to do little but work. Yet he reeled off trips and accomplishments ("I've published two books and have three more written in my head") that he merely considered to be part of his job.

David Rockefeller, chairman of The Chase Manhattan Bank, told *The New Yorker* "I can't imagine a more interesting job than mine. . . . The bank has dealings with everything. There is no field of activity it isn't involved in. It's a springboard for whatever interests one may have in any direction." And Barbara Walters once told a reporter, "I'm doing what I absolutely love. . . . I have the best job that anyone could have. . . . I have the opportunity to meet everyone, to interview everyone."[2]

The Diffuse Workaholic. This third kind of workaholic is likely to have "fingers in lots of pies" and "several balls in the air" whether at work or not. These people may change jobs and fields fairly frequently. Their pursuits are more scattered than those of integrated workaholics. One Wall Street executive exemplified this approach particularly well. "I'm hyper during the day," he explained. "I have a kind of short attention span where a lot of things turn me on, and then, after a short period of time, I will drop them."

Similarly, one woman concedes "this job doesn't fill my time." So she resorts to filling her twenty-hour days with work for over a dozen committees, task forces, charitable organizations, civic groups, and community boards.

The Intense Workaholic. The fourth type of

workaholic pursues leisure activities with the same passion, sense of purpose, and pace as he pursues work. A hobby just becomes "a job of a different kind." Recognizing this, one writer has warned that hobbies can be dangerous because workaholics will pursue them with "the same intensity and preoccupation as they do their work." As one woman workaholic told me, "I love sports. . . . I'm as avid about those as I am about working." She believes that "anybody who's very intense in business is also intense in their other pursuits." For example, more than one person in my sample was a marathoner, applying the same energy and exactitude toward training, clocking times, and completing difficult courses as toward their careers.

Alex Lewyt, who founded the vacuum cleaner company that bears his name, was profiled by *The New York Times*. Since Lewyt never took vacations, his doctor told him that he was a prime candidate for a heart attack and urged him to get a hobby. But he began collecting watches and clocks so obsessively that the doctor finally told him to lay off the timepieces, too.

So now we know how to identify a workaholic: It's that blur of a person rushing by with the overflowing briefcase, dictating into a recorder, checking the time, and munching on a sandwich. How did these people get that way?

3
Workaholics:
How Do They Get That Way?

*I'm no smarter than anybody else, I just
need less sleep.*
—Sonny Werblin

Just exactly how do people get addicted to their
work? No one knows for sure, but it is possible to
speculate a little about the causes. Workaholics are
not born with an appointment book and a Cross pen
in their hands. Nor do they suddenly emerge full-
blown as work addicts in their first jobs. As with any
psychological phenomenon, the seeds of workaholism are planted early.

Of course workaholism looks a little different in
children than it does in adults; few kids scurry to
catch Eastern's 7 A.M. air shuttle. It pays to observe
young children at play. Games are not just child's
play, but sometimes serious business. As "Saturday
Night Live" star Gilda Radner reveals, "The games I
made up as a child were all work-oriented. They
were me in sales, selling sticks in the backyard. I

once heard my mother say, 'You'd sell ice in the wintertime.' And the expression stuck in my mind. So in the wintertime, I'd go out in my leggings and my coat and chip big pieces of ice and pretend I was selling them." Radner also recalls, "My father was in the hotel business . . . I'd go down there with him and they'd let me learn to work the switchboard. I'd sit there and play with it. So of course I continued that game at home. I used to use my tennis shoes. I'd put the shoelaces in my tennis shoes in the same way an operator would work a switchboard."

Other children actually turn their play into paying work. Lemonade stands are commonplace, but some kids start play groups for smaller children, run sidewalk carnivals, or cash in everything from returnable soda bottles to recyclable beer cans and the beetles and bugs that are the bane of gardeners. (I should know, I did them all.) A little later, they turn to more lucrative pursuits: selling more Girl Scout cookies, Christmas cards, and magazine subscriptions than anyone else on the block. Sometimes, too, outdoor work, housework, or other pursuits prove immediately profitable, as the existence of teenage tycoons attests.

What is most telling about this money-making mania is that financial need is not a factor. I devoted endless hours to my games and schemes although all my basic needs were met and my weekly allowance was perfectly adequate to keep me supplied with comic books, bubble gum, and ice cream cones.

Once children start school, workaholism is more readily recognizable. Guidance counselors may abhor it, but teachers adore it. Soon-to-be-workaholics take copious, careful notes in every class and cram their assignment books with projects and plans. They do not have to be told to do their homework. Rather, they race home and finish it fast. They are then free to turn their attention to extra credit projects: collecting and labeling autumn leaves; writing book reports; looking things up in the dictionary and encyclopedia; making models of the human heart for a science fair.

Later still, they become living, breathing examples of overcommitted organization children. They squeeze school and schoolwork into an overcrowded schedule of art lessons, dancing classes, swimming instruction, acting classes, piano lessons, Scout meetings, religious instruction, Little League games, orthodontist appointments, and the like. Lacking little appointment books, they manage to keep their schedules straight by consulting complicated kitchen calendars and depending heavily upon their parents or parent-substitutes (housekeepers, baby sitters, grandparents).

While all workaholics are driven, some are also pushed. "Most of the time, children's workaholism is a direct extrapolation of the home style," explains Laurence A. Susser, a pediatrician-turned-psychiatrist who practices in New York City and New Rochelle. "Parents start sending messages about their expectations early on." They might play classical music before the baby's birth in an attempt to create the next Mozart or buy baseball bats before the baby is out of diapers. Such parents seem to "require" their children's achievements, and they reinforce this by rewarding the accomplishments and, sometimes, little else. Monica Bauer of Xerox, an only child, recalls that her parents were ambitious for her. "Their expectation for me was 'We anticipate that you will exceed and excel.'" Similarly, Dr. Elizabeth Whelan remembers that her parents did, in fact, urge her to aim for and apply to Yale and Harvard, where she earned her graduate degrees.

When such "encouragement" becomes extreme, children can start to worry that love will be withdrawn if they fail to bring home straight As or don't get admitted to the college of their parents' choice. The standards become even harder to meet and failure grows all the more frightening as children fulfill or surpass their parents' ever-increasing expectations and must aim for more. This pattern proves to be self-perpetuating. As workaholics work even harder to gain approval, that approval becomes even more elusive. As with the proverb, "Do a little more each day than everyone expects and soon everyone will expect more," so it is with young workaholics: The more they accomplish, the more they're expected to do.

Seeing parental love as contingent on achievement instead of unconditional surely spurs progress, but it may also be the source of workaholics' selfdoubts. Graphic artist and magazine design director Milton Glaser works hard, he says, because "essentially, it's a demonstration of my potency, my power." His long list of credits has won him wide acclaim, but what he cites as rewards are "the approval of parents, admiration of peers, and the acknowledgment of the public."

Success is self-perpetuating, but the promise of failure is even more propelling and compelling. One man traced the onset of his work pattern to a confluence of childhood circumstances.

> When I was seven years old, my parents owned a candy store in Brooklyn. We were one of the few Jewish families in a very Christian, very hostile environment. My father, who was a product of Europe and The Depression, was very afraid I would never escape this existence. He told me that I was going to be a failure. And, that, in combination with getting beat up every day on the way to school, made me draw upon all the resources a seven-year-old boy has available and I decided to get very smart, very quickly.

Thereafter, he spent a safe and studious adolescence, getting into academic honor societies while his peers were getting into trouble. As he reflects now, after years of analysis, "By being productive and 'good' while avoiding the storms of adolescence, I managed to get a pat on the back and to miss a lot of pain."

Another source of motivation for most workaholics is fear. *They fear failure.* Not having failed, they have not had to learn that failure is not the end of the world. And the successes they've realized make failure all the more foreboding. So any joy over a triumph is also delight at not having failed. *They fear boredom.* Suggest they take a week-long trip and they regard you with disbelief. "What would I do?" they ask. *They fear laziness.* This is most interesting.

Appearances to the contrary, many workaholics suspect that deep down inside they are actually lazy.
They keep driving themselves because they think
that if they let up, their natural laziness will do them
in. In *You Can't Go Home Again*, Thomas Wolfe
echoes this point:

> I've got an idea that a lot of the work in this world
> gets done by lazy people. That's the reason they
> work—because they're so lazy—It's this way: You
> work because you're afraid not to. You work be-
> cause you have to drive yourself to such a fury to
> begin. That part's just hell!! It's so hard to get
> started that once you do you're afraid of slipping
> back. You'd rather do anything than go through
> that agony again—so you keep going till you
> couldn't stop even if you wanted to. . . . Then
> people say you're a glutton for work, but it isn't so.
> It's laziness—just plain, damned simple laziness,
> that's all.

Then, too, the model of a parent in perpetual
motion may instill guilt over any signs of sloth in the
child. One woman spent childhood summers by the
seashore. Other people, she recalls, thought her
mother was a widow since her father was seldom
with them. But "once in a great while his big white
body would show up on the beach. I used to feel
tremendous guilt that he was slaving away in New
York while we were luxuriating in the sun."

Parents who happen to be workaholics serve as
models for their offspring to imitate and emulate. Quite
a few of the people I interviewed saw signs of incipi-
ent workaholism in their children. Workaholism is
probably transmitted more indirectly than directly;

none of the parents interviewed were aware of or would admit to telling their children to "put time to good use." Indeed, they were neither pleased nor proud to see their children following in their footsteps. One journalist recalled her father telling her and her siblings, "I should be a lesson to all of you not to do this with your lives." But the real message comes across by means of observation and absorption. The same woman attributes her own work pattern to her workaholic father. She works hard herself and shares his disdain for those who don't. She explains, "I think my father has such tremendous drive that it spills over to other people and you measure your sense of worth by being productive."

Psychodynamic processes also give rise to workaholism. The pattern underlying workaholism is the obsessive-compulsive neurosis. In his classic work *Neurotic Styles,* David Shapiro typifies obsessive-compulsives as very rigid in their thinking; sharp, narrowed, and focused in their attention; endlessly active; concerned with being in control; and apt to engage in ritualistic behaviors as though they were "living machines." According to some psychotherapists, people overcome anxiety with a variety of methods, one of which is obsessive overwork. Obsessive rituals—whether related to working, washing, or cleaning—are a major source of reassurance and security for the anxious. These patterns are set in childhood and often stem from whatever people were praised for as children. Compulsive behavior starts early and sticks. One New Jersey real estate developer continually flicked specks of lint from his suit and cigarette ashes from his desk as we spoke. He mentioned his tendency to write far too many notes to himself: "I'll make a list of things to do and I'll find I have seven lists." Upon reflection, he realized that he had shown a similar propensity from grade school to graduate school. "I used to take so many notes I didn't have time to study for tests."

The Type A behavior pattern corresponds quite closely to that of the obsessive-compulsive and probably to workaholics. Two San Francisco cardiologists, Doctors Meyer Friedman and Ray Rosenman, discovered and defined Type A behavior as a "complex of personality traits, including excessive competitive drive, aggressiveness, impatience, and a harrying sense of time urgency."[1] David C. Glass, professor of psychology at the City University of New York has concluded that "the Type A person works hard and fast to succeed, and in striving toward his goals, he suppresses feelings, such as fatigue, that might interfere with his performance. Type As get angry if someone or something gets in the way of their success. I submit that all of these traits suggest a person who rises to master challenges out of need to control his world."[2]

The quest to achieve control is not simply a contest but a brutal, futile battle. Workaholics' cluttered calendars represent an attempt to "beat the clock." Their lists are but "a way to organize the unorganizable," according to David Wallechinsky, who should know: He's co-author of *The Book of Lists*. This perceived need for organization creates a tendency to cram all objectives into a stable, predictable, and inadequate amount of time in order to achieve a semblance of control. One lawyer, for instance, indicated that of all the "perks," pay, praise, and prestige that accompanied his election to partnership in his firm, what he valued most was simply having more control over his work.

Workaholics can, however, lose sight of what is and what is not within their control. They become annoyed when two events they wish to attend are held simultaneously. They also respond rather poorly to violations of their ordinarily orderly existence—even to something so simple as the newspaper's not being outside the door at the customary time.

Control—or the illusion thereof—is vitally important to workaholics. To understand how important it is, you need only listen to them try to explain a loss of (or at least a lack of) control. The president of a small philanthropic foundation said:

> People simply go to seed when they have nothing to do. People complain when there's too much work to do but this is more often than not the good-natured complaining of people who know that they can cope with it, whereas others wouldn't, so there's pride in the fact that stuff's all piled up.

An ad agency head who commonly completes commitments for twenty to thirty clients at a time admits, "I complain all the time, knowing that I take them on myself. I seek them."

Part of the reason for seeking new challenges is to provide new experiences. While some people prefer a stable, static environment, workaholics crave continual stimulation. This leads to a physiological explanation of workaholics' work involvement. Their reluctance to rest relies upon their physical resilience. While others may experience an energy shortage, workaholics suffer from a surfeit. They are a hearty crew and their stamina sets them apart. They recall being the same way throughout their lives. One woman remarked that she was always active as a child and never needed naps, much to her mother's dismay. Needing so little sleep annoys anyone they live with and astounds everyone they know. Someone telephoned me not long ago at 10:00 on a Saturday morning. She apologized and asked if she had awakened me: "You never *seem* to sleep but I figure you must."

4

Workaholics:

At Work

*But precisely because he works so hard, it's
hard to figure out exactly what he's doing
wrong.*
—A New York psychiatrist

Once they move into the world of work, workaholics find themselves in their element. Even if they
were not the best and the brightest students or were
too involved in extracurriculars to qualify as
"grinds", once at work, they often excel. They can do
more, and do it better and faster, than almost anyone
else. They throw themselves into things; they absorb
new facts, figures, or fields rapidly and work hard
and well. Often they quickly rise in the hierarchy
without a lot of maneuvering simply because they
work harder, longer, and smarter than anyone else.

As the ad opposite suggests, many companies
covet or collect workaholics. But there has also been
some organizational concern about work addicts.
The typical view, as expressed by Robert D. Caplan

ADMINISTRATIVE MANAGEMENT TRAINEE

We are looking for a competitive "workaholic" for our administration operation. Must be interested in learning and doing labor law administrative management and be practically imaginative to do professional recruiting. LLB or MBA with BS in Economics or Engineering required. Must possess loyalty and presence which commands respect in community and company. Starting salary to $20,000. Send resume stating employment and salary history.

From *The Wall Street Journal*, January 9, 1979.

and Kenneth W. Jones of the University of Michigan's Institute for Social Research, is that workaholics "contribute to their organizations at some cost to their own mental and physical health."[1] Most organizations, however, are willing to chance such individual risks in the name of collective gain.

Indeed, many jobs seem to require exactly the devotion and sacrifice of personal lives that social scientists denounce. In an attempt to keep productivity up and personnel costs down, some companies create jobs that are too big for one person to tackle, jobs that beg for workaholics to fill them. This pattern is truer at the top than at the bottom of the pyramid. Andrew D. Hart, executive vice president of Russell Reynolds Associates, a leading executive recruiting firm, maintains that "the higher you go up the ladder, the harder people have to work." Many companies claim that they would like to "clone" more workaholics; they certainly are assumed to be excellent executives.

But there is another side to the workaholic at work. In fact, one of the most startling findings of my entire study was that some workaholics may be among the world's worst workers. These work addicts suffer few ill effects themselves, but wind up doing enormous damage to the companies and organizations for which they labor long and hard. They prove to be a high cost to the company, both directly (who else pays for extra shifts of secretaries?) and indirectly.

They may create a pressure-cooker atmosphere in which subordinates—and even superiors—burn out or burn up. Workaholics simultaneously delegate too little: A vice president for facilities who prices the cost of a single can of paint is keeping overly close tabs on things. And they demand too much. Although most deny it, they expect everyone to show the same dedication to duty that they do, and they sneer at those who don't or won't. It is also possible that they sometimes accomplish far less than they think.

Workaholics may actually be incapable of setting limits on their work and deciding what does and what does not have to be done. They can't say "No" to anything. They feel that they cannot do enough. As one woman said, "As long as I work until I'm exhausted, I feel I'm not wasting my life." And "good enough" is not in their vocabularies. Rather, they believe that even if something is already good,

it can be—it has *got* to be—made better. Long hours
can lead them to overdo things or do them over.
Worst of all, more than one workaholic has worked
very hard on the *wrong* things. Believing in the
adage "When in doubt, work," some workaholics
don't work smarter, they just work harder.

Whether they recognize it or not, workaholics
often have difficulty dealing with people, a situation
that is particularly apparent when the workaholic is
a boss. What organizations require from their managers is the ability to work with and through other
people; it's impossible to run a large organization
alone. But some workaholics try to do just that. They
can demoralize and demotivate their subordinates by
denying them the opportunity to do anything on their
own. A case in point is a risk arbitrageur who
"has only one assistant to whom he gives any trading
discretion. The rest of his forty or so employees follow his instructions." As he told *The Wall Street
Journal*, "I've learned it's best to do it yourself."[2]

A woman who is a vice president in the staff
department of a large commercial bank said, "This
job doesn't fill my time. . . . They can ask me to do
something here that they want in a month. I can do it
in two days. . . . I work quickly, I can grasp
quickly, learn, take over, and get the job done." As a
result, she feels, "I'm much too fast-moving for this
institution. I could be doing ten times more than I'm
doing." She continued:

> I really enjoy working with people very much, but I
> really don't want 200 clerks reporting to me. I
> mean, I've had people reporting to me here and I've

never had any problem with it. But I'd just as soon be more on my own at this point. I really like the challenge of thinking about what I want to do and of being able to go and hire really good people [as consultants] to get the job done. I just think it's drudgery being in charge of an operating department.

To maintain the myth that they are irreplaceable and indispensable—that only they can do the job— some workaholics withhold essential information from their subordinates or co-workers. They may even avoid important out-of-town meetings or social engagements with clients for fear that some of their functions will be taken over by others or that a superior may come to realize that their efforts are not as crucial as they had led the boss to believe. Workaholics balk at what they term "interference" from people who have a perfect right to "interfere." One copywriter, for example, objected to "letting anybody else get their grubby fingers" on any ad he creates. The people he had in mind? Why, clients and creative directors.

Workaholics are terrible delegators. They resist relinquishing responsibility and authority, and when they must, they meddle anyway. They may even annoy those who are not under their direct supervision. Should such interference ruin the results, workaholics are apt to conclude that their original reluctance was warranted. A creative supervisor at one well-known Madison Avenue ad agency is bright and breezy, the very picture of the Harvard M.B.A. that he is. As he became aware that others in

the agency were avoiding opportunities to be as-
signed to his accounts, he made a conscious attempt
to change his ways: "I've tried to become a better
delegator. I'm trying to give people a lot of responsibility and to give them very high standards to meet,
but I'm also trying to constantly look over their
shoulders."

This ad man has identified another deficiency
of workaholics: They demand a lot. Another
banker acknowledges how tough a boss she is: "I do
make demands on people. . . . I am a perfectionist.
If people don't perform and pull their weight here,
they don't stay here. The minute someone doesn't
pull their weight, it becomes immediately apparent.
I don't react well and I don't react with a great deal of
patience."

Paradoxically, even if they try to do everything
themselves, they simultaneously expect everyone
else to work as hard as they do. They look down on
people who don't work hard, but their standards for
hard work are often unreasonably stringent. One law
partner watched an associate head for the door at 10
P.M. and told him, "You'll never be a good lawyer."

Workaholics will demand devotion and dedication to the job even when their subordinates are at
home asleep. An aide to one New York politician
described the predicament: He would be awakened
in the middle of the night by a phone call from the
boss, who would immediately begin a rapid-fire
burst of instructions without pausing to explain. The
aide complained, "He expects you to have been
thinking about what he's been thinking about."

According to *The Power Broker*, Robert Moses, the man responsible for many of New York's parks and highways who is still going strong in his 90s, "kept lists of his aides' phone numbers, and he used that list around the clock, frequently at 2 or 3 A.M. If they went out at night, they had to leave phone numbers at which they could be reached, and they became accustomed to having ushers search them out in darkened theatres to ask them to come to the manager's office for an urgent phone call. If Moses needed a man when the man was in Florida, the man was summoned home."

Another attorney is notorious for working his people beyond their limits. Each of his last two secretaries quit: One entered a hospital suffering from nervous exhaustion and the other had a nervous breakdown. His present secretary says, "The little joke going around the office is wondering how long it will be before I have a nervous breakdown!"

But she has it easy: When her boss wants to work until 4 or 5 A.M., she is relieved and replaced by a second secretary no later than midnight. His young law associates, however, are expected to stay there with him until the wee hours and, of course, be at work the next morning. Furthermore, should an associate dare to complain of fatigue, the partner is liable to launch into a little lecture ("Three hours' sleep should be more than enough for anyone") and to take their "unwillingness to work" into account on their performance appraisals.

Such behavior is not restricted to politicians' smoke-filled rooms or Wall Street suites. Hal

Holding, 25, of Palo Alto, California, spent two years
managing the largest paperback bookstore in the Bay
area. His biggest headache was the realization that "I
couldn't expect other people to work as long or as
hard as I did." His wife, Beverly, who worked there
with him, explained, "Management loved him, but
everybody else resented him because he was has-
sling them. He couldn't understand why anyone
would be mad when he was just asking them to do
what they were there to do."

Even competent colleagues can have trouble
keeping up with the pace and standards workaholics
set. One lawyer's secretary sadly stated, "Sometimes
my best isn't good enough." A woman who once
worked as secretary for Dr. Florence Haseltine, the
Yale University gynecologist, admitted, "I couldn't
keep up with her. She amazed me. She was trying to
do everything all the time. Her mind would constantly be going on a lot of things and she'd never
lose sight of what she was working on."

Workaholics tend to be critical and contemptuous of co-workers. The disdain is often undeserved
and particularly petty. Every absence is construed as
an offense and every illness is inexcusable. One advertising executive I interviewed supervised several
people. He apparently scrutinized and obviously
criticized their attendance records, observing,
"People are constantly calling in sick. Any little illness they magnify in their minds. They can't wait to
call in sick."

Workaholics display little interest in and great
intolerance for the personal lives of assistants and

associates. They seldom ask, "How's the family?" and don't listen to the answer, if they do. Another advertising executive sneered at the "self-improvement smorgasbord . . . everything from EST to biofeedback" so many of his colleagues were into. He also had little empathy for a colleague whose personal life had undergone some turmoil. He saw the situation strictly in financial terms: After "an expensive divorce" his colleague had to move in with a woman "for economic reasons." Similarly, a lawyer in a large firm had great difficulty dealing with or even describing the situation of a widower he knew who was resuming a single social life in middle age: "All of a sudden his sideburns got longer, he got a convertible, and started taking long weekends, going to resorts."

Workaholics may be more interested in the Selectric than the secretary behind it. After five years on the job, one secretary returned from lunch one day minus the thick-framed glasses she'd always worn, having exchanged them for her first pair of contact lenses. Her boss—a woman—was quick to notice the change in her secretary's appearance, but her interest was all business. She exclaimed, "You don't have your glasses on. How are you going to type for me?"

Another surprise is that while some workaholics hold others in disdain, their own legendary effectiveness and efficiency is sometimes lacking. Dr. Susser said, "There's a myth that the workaholic is efficient. Not true. It takes him twelve hours to do what others can do in only eight. . . . Everybody thinks that what they took twelve to do can't be done in eight." One executive who has had as many as four secretaries at one time now has none. Instead of spending her time attending to that which only she can do, she now spends some of her time typing, which almost anyone can do. Even their beloved lists may cost them some efficiency. Dr. Whelan, the epidemiologist and author, begins each day "with a detailed list of everything to be accomplished." However, as she freely admits, her main time-waster is looking for or rewriting the lists she misplaces.

In some cases, the important work just doesn't get done. The secretary to the president of a New York City philanthropic foundation notes that her boss has a tendency to "slough off" routine chores and concentrate on what he wants to do instead of what needs to be done. "He'd much rather be out in the field doing exciting things—who wouldn't?— and sometimes develops a huge backlog."

Even their seemingly inexhaustible energy supply poses some problems. Workaholics may try to do everything, instead of setting and sticking to priorities. One company president candidly confessed, "Some things which are unimportant are fascinating and some things which are important are terrible drudgery, so I never get around to them."

The routine and repetition that comprise "drudgery" are inherent, to some degree, in almost any job. Requiring continual challenges and continual stimulation, this situation may render workaholics relatively useless. While they are adept at developing their own new tasks, they then run the risk of creating new problems as well. As one man said, "If I didn't have a problem to solve, I would develop something else to solve." In other words, those who enjoy fighting fires might also start some or, at least, fan their flames.

Workaholics may also lose perspective, the result of the narrowness that comes from focusing too intently. Sometimes work addicts just don't see the forest for the trees. One headhunter explained that while clients would welcome a workaholic candidate who was "emotionally stable, . . . what they don't want is someone who's such a genius on semiconductors that he forgets what the semiconductors conduct."

Another outcome of their intense focus is that workaholics may substitute personal objectives for organizational ones. As the late humorist Robert Benchley reportedly observed, "The secret of my incredible energy and efficiency in getting work done is a simple one. . . . anyone can do any amount of work, providing it isn't the work he is *supposed* to be doing." In some cases, of course, the priorities that workaholics perceive, though seemingly at odds with those of their organizations, may prove preferable in the long run. The intent of their focus may be visionary. One noted researcher suspects that being fired is a fate that frequently befalls workaholics simply because they won't subscribe to mass standards. She cites her own experience as an example: "I was the head of the department of pharmacology at a fairly large drug house at a fairly early age. One day I was fired. The chairman of the board had told the top company officers that they'd be fired if I wasn't let go." The reason? She had asked that a certain new drug be withdrawn from clinical trial. Her caution proved correct: That drug was later found to cause tragic birth defects.

But there is also the chance that their focus is not so much foresighted as fixated. Workaholics have been criticized for being rigid—proceeding in the same, tried-and-true ritualistic way—rather than spontaneous. They may then miss those opportunities that don't fit into their schemes or schedules.

To workaholics, schedules are sacrosanct. But only their *own* schedules count; they don't accommodate anyone else's. As an associate of a consultant I interviewed explained, "You fit in with his schedule."

You might not want to work for producer Shelly Gross for that very reason. Despite his staff, there's a typewriter by his desk for those times when something just won't wait: "I don't like things to drag." Similarly, he has no hesitation about telling a staff member to get off the phone to take care of something he wants done: "I can do it, I'm the boss."

Hal Holding, who stopped managing his bookstore and started selling books as a travelling representative for a New York-based publisher, admits that he gets impatient and intolerant when he has to spend time with an account who likes to sit and talk. Holding concedes that he may rush some of them and drop those that waste too much of his time.

These actions and reactions of workaholics often have serious negative effects in an organization. First of all, they often make everyone else look like slackers. "My boss' secretary says I write as much business in a day as many of the other reps write in a week," said Holding. "One of them said to me, 'Stop working so hard. You make the rest of us look bad.' "

Another person I interviewed, a social worker, described a job in which "you had to put down how much time you put in each day. The first couple of weeks I had been putting in fifteen hours over the forty hours [we were supposed to work]. My boss didn't like that." Of course, such bosses may merely be sincerely concerned. The same social worker continued, "He sat down with me a couple of times and said 'You're going to kill yourself! You're going to get burned out!' So I ended up not putting those hours down on the sheet and I kept working those hours and never told him."

Also, workaholics don't necessarily set a good example. If talented subordinates think that the only route to success is the workaholics' way, then those who do not wish to emulate them may look elsewhere and leave. A 1976 *Boston Globe* profile of Edwin Land, the founder and chairman of Polaroid, described his day and its sometimes deleterious effects:

> Land works harder and longer than most men half
> his age. . . . He rises at 5:30 every morning in his
> Brattle Street residence and 'paces around' until
> 7:00, the earliest he feels he can rightfully call as
> sociates to make suggestions and ask ques
> tions. . . . his intense personal drive and disdain
> for people who work 9-to-5 days creates problems,

too. He wants his associates to push as hard as he does, and, as a result, many drop out.

Finally, workaholics who exaggerate their own indispensability can impede the interests of the organization. Superbly qualified subordinates who might become rivals are purposely not hired. Workaholics also engage in empire building: They take on too much work, don't delegate duties even where it would be appropriate, and relinquish the duties and privileges of any previous positions only with reluctance even when they have been promoted.

At the very least, workaholics tend not to cooperate or communicate with colleagues. Since work is crucial to their sense of self, they may use it to seek approval and admiration. Any criticism will thus meet with more hostility and resentment than it might otherwise elicit; any suggestions are likely to be construed as meddling and ignored. The workaholic may assert his importance by steadfastly maintaining that he "just can't take time off," a statement designed to simultaneously indicate his loyalty to the job and suggest that he is far more vital to the enterprise than he in fact is.

At the negative extreme, the workaholic may always be out for himself, unwilling to subordinate his individual goals to the good of the organization as a whole. And he may be jealous, hostile, resentful and overly competitive. Some companies indicate that they are starting to face up to these negative consequences. Jay I. Bennett, Revlon's senior vice president for personnel and industrial relations, finds workaholism neither necessary nor desirable. He and his staff do not look for workaholics when filling positions, although he seems to expect and demand the dedication characteristic of work-aholics. He makes no bones about the fact that business pressures often warrant working long hours. Revlon people, Bennett maintains, "must be prepared to put the time in. . . . I think you have to differentiate between a workaholic and a very responsible person. Such self-motivated people are the best people you could find."

But there seems to be a very fine line between the highly motivated, energetic person and the workaholic. Employers may *say* that they want people with balanced lives and outside interests, they may pretend that workaholics are not welcome—but in fact they still encourage work-aholic tendencies. Many executives are sought above all for their energy and willingness to work. As Hal Higdon states in *The Business Healers*, a chronicle of the consulting world, "A lot of consultants are simply compulsive workers. . . . The most valuable asset that a consultant brings into any assignment is his own intensity. Management consulting firms carefully seek as employees individuals who possess this particular attribute."

Gerard Roche, who heads Heidrick and Struggles, another leading executive search firm, concurs. "Somebody without a high energy level can't make it in top management." Still, as he concedes, there are 9-to-5 types holding down top jobs at more than one major multinational. "But," he emphasizes, "they're a rarity.'' More often than not, Roche explains, such people are protected both by those who preceded them and those who report to them.

And while it can be difficult to work for a workaholic, many managers still buy the stereotype and think it would not be nearly so bad to have one work for them. Richard Armour summed up this situation best in a poem entitled, "Take My Word":

> A recent word is workaholic,
> One caught by something diabolic.
> But dangerous though it may be,
> I'd like to have one work for me.*

The truth is that workaholics are probably much better suited to entrepreneurial ventures or jobs that are not part of a bureaucratic organization. Workaholism seems to be very effective when you're trying to make a go of a mom-and-pop operation. The same traits that make them terrible bosses in an organization make them terrific entrepreneurs. But the problems start when success arrives—when the previously small operation blossoms into an organization and the workaholic has to manage a number of people. Founders sometimes flounder under such circumstances; for many, the transition required is tantamount to a transformation. But it can be made.

In 1973, Steven Poses, a bearded, bushy-haired, and friendly man now in his early 30s, opened a restaurant, Frog, in Philadelphia. It was such a suc-

---

* From *The Wall Street Journal,* December 29, 1978. Copyright © 1978 Dow Jones & Company, Inc. Reprinted by permission.

cess that in 1977 he opened a second restaurant, The Commissary, where our interview was held. This restaurant combines country charm and casual chic; utterly wonderful food is served cafeteria-style. His clientele includes those ubiquitous ladies who lunch and scores of Philadelphia lawyers (recognizable by the yellow legal pads they carry), who choose this as a fairly quick alternative to the more mundane McDonald's and other fast-food outlets nearby.

In seven years, Steve Poses' staff has grown from none to nearly 200. He recalls "that point when I had to learn to start depending upon other people" as "the crucial turning point." Until then, he thought that "if nobody showed up, I'd still be able to do it all," but he realizes that he no longer can. His first employee, who is still with him, acknowledges that "delegating responsibility was a hard lesson for Steve to learn. It took him a long time to learn to give others the responsibility they need." But now he gives his boss fairly high marks: "He's able to bring a number of qualities together. He certainly knows about food, he knows how to manage people, and he has a sense of style." Poses apparently doesn't expect twenty-four-hour dedication: The only time he called this employee during the middle of the night was when one of the restaurants was on fire.

5
Workaholics:
At Home

*I may be a lousy father and a lousy
husband, but when Merrill Lynch needs
me, I'm here.*
—A stockbroker

If you think workaholics are sometimes difficult
to work with, just wait until you try to live with one.
Of course, you'll hardly ever see a workaholic at
home; they are apt to be absent and away more often
than they acknowledge or admit. When workaholics
do stay home, they're either working or thinking
about work. You may think you're having a conversation with them when suddenly—in the middle of
your sentence—they pull out a pocket tape recorder
and start dictating "things to do" or they produce a
pack of index cards and start scribbling. So although
they are physically in the house, often they might as
well not be. As more than one family member knows,
the absence of the workaholic is often more meaningful and more memorable than the presence.

Any attempts to rectify this imbalance tend to be

more half-hearted than heartfelt and are also apt to come too late. Parents may truly intend to spend more time with their children "someday" only to find that their children are grown and gone by then. One man expressed sincere regret over the rearing of his children: "The biggest mistake I ever made was neglecting my children. The kids were brought up without my being home. I used to leave in the morning when it was dark and they weren't up and come home when they were sleeping."

While the workaholics I interviewed spoke of success only in relation to their work, their feelings of failure were usually family-related. For a work addict, family life simply cannot compete with the office. The ex-wife of an economist summarized the situation leading to her divorce with a statement that is as sad as it is succinct: "My husband was married to his work." Indeed, this set of circumstances is so commonplace that it prompted Mortimer R. Feinberg, a New York psychologist, to coin the term "corporate bigamist" to describe those who are, in fact, more dedicated and devoted to their jobs than to their spouses. After surveying several hundred male executives and their nonworking wives, Feinberg found that such statements, alibis, and excuses as "I'll make it up to them" or "I'm doing it all for them" rang rather false. As the wife of one physician explained, "My husband's patients always came first and [after forty-one years of marriage] still do!"

Dr. Harvey L. Ruben, a New Haven psychiatrist, told *The Philadelphia Inquirer*, "Often we're not aware of what we're doing to ourselves and our families. Our denial can be fantastic." A case in point appeared in *Esquire*, where it was reported that Fred Smith, founder of Federal Express Corporation, works long and late and frequently travels one or two nights a week. The interviewer asked Mrs. Smith how she felt about her husband's absence those one or two nights a week. She snapped back, "You mean three or four nights a week."

Similarly, an attorney I interviewed expressed regret about the amount of time he spent away from his wife and young daughters. As a partner in a leading international law firm, he frequently finds himself in rather remote parts of the world, where, he says, "I call whenever I can, but, very often, I'm in places without telephones." Despite his protestations, he may spend next to no time with them when he is in town. He has been known to head for a hotel close to the courthouse during particularly tough trials. There he holes up with his associates for an orgy of work. He explains, "I've actually moved out of the house, moved into a hotel and have not gone home for weeks at a time."

The evidence is still inconclusive as to whether involvement in work inevitably and invariably exists at the cost of involvement at home. Lotte Bailyn, the M.I.T. psychologist, has argued that individuals possess a finite amount of energy that, when invested in work, is then unavailable to the family. But another line of reasoning, espoused by Douglas T. Hall of Northwestern University and Samuel Rabinowitz of New York University, states that the more involved and satisfied people are at work, the more active they

will be in other areas as well.[1] It is indeed possible
for involvement and satisfaction at work to carry
over and improve other aspects of living. Several
people commented that their workaholic spouses'
enthusiasm was exciting and inspiring. They felt
shortchanged only by the limited amount of time
they had together. The scarcity of time together may
be a smart strategy in itself. One woman workaholic
felt that her home life was enhanced by her hectic
work schedule. She and her husband had their own
lives and interests and, as she explained, "We aren't
together all the time so we're never bored when we
are."

But while some families may benefit from a
workaholic's involvement in work, more seem to suffer because of it. "Somebody said I was married to
my job," Golda Meir remarked in a *New York Times*
interview held not long before her death. "My children suffered at various times, but when they got
older, they understood. As for my husband, he was a
wonderful human being. Bad luck that he married
me."

Many of the workaholics I interviewed paid little more than lip service to their families. A leading
advertising executive I interviewed, for example,
claimed to be close to his kids. Yet his behavior belied his words: despite ample opportunity to do so,
he did not mention them for the first thirty-five minutes of a forty-five-minute interview. By the time he
did get around to talking about his children, I was
startled to hear he had any. Similarly, the editor of a
well-known weekly news magazine could recall

with precision the number of hours he had worked the week before (80) and the number of years he had been with the publication (21½), but he could not remember how long he had been married ("I've been married to the same woman for . . . uh . . . a long time").

Workaholism can represent an attempt to avoid the conflict between home and office. One need not even have a family to experience such conflict. Single workaholics frequently find that their social lives deteriorate into a series of broken dates. Furthermore, sudden and repeated cancellations of dinner dates or squash games mean that future invitations will tend to be few.

In resolving such conflicts, work usually wins. Adam Johnson (a pseudonym) is an advertising executive whose corporate climb entailed several cross-country moves. When asked what problems his commitment to his career had posed, he did not mention any, and, indeed, did not seem aware of any. He explained, "I made the decision a while ago—and my wife agreed with me—that my professional life would take precedence."

Still, most workaholics try to make conscientious attempts to spend time at home. But watch what they do: One man said that his wife had "basically turned our bedroom into an office. Now she wants to get a home Vydec machine, but that's where I draw the line." Often, they've strewn the dining room table with papers or locked themselves inside a spare room, unwilling to be interrupted. The wife of an advertising executive I'll call Stan Michaels never

knows when he will be home but can always tell
when he is:

> I know he is home by interruptions, complaints,
> and the many things he delegates to me to handle.
> You can never forget that he is around. . . . He
> complains about a million little things: "Why are
> the garbage cans still out? Why are all the lights
> on? Why do I let the children do such and such?
> Why are there fingerprints on the wall?

Or else they're trying to do half a dozen things at
once: talking on the telephone while watching the
news and reading the mail.

Or take a look at them when they're trying to
spend time doing something that their spouses or
children want to do. One man would dutifully accompany his wife to the opera, ballet, or even the
movies only to fall sound asleep as soon as he sank
into the seat. Another workaholic decided to take his
kids to sports events on Saturdays and Sundays, although he hadn't the slightest interest in them. So
there he sat, in cold stands or overheated bleachers,
with one child on each side of him and a stack of
business reports and other reading in his lap.

As partners, workaholics are not much better.
Guy Lafleur, a star of the Montreal Canadiens hockey
team, told a reporter for The New York Times that,
after traveling with the team 100 days a year or more
"you get so used to being served, so you're very
spoiled. You go back home, there's a big difference.
You think you're on the road. [Snapping his fingers]
Bring me this, bring me that. Your wife just goes
mad."

Workaholics who can't bear to lose control over the smallest detail at work readily relinquish this role at home. Not surprisingly, middle-aged men shirk (or as they would say "delegate") household work. Said one, "I try to do as little as possible." Said another, "My wife is convinced that I'm helpless around anything mechanical, which is an opinion I studiously cultivated in her." And another admitted, "I don't have responsibilities, really; at least I don't assume them." It is, indeed, difficult to imagine exactly how little such men actually do around the house. Dick Vermeil, the Philadelphia football coach, was more candid than most. "I don't even write a check," he said. "I don't think about things like that."

Such "delegation" is demeaning and demanding, so, housework can be a source of considerable domestic discussion and dissension. One man said, "That's a problem area. I decided my wife would take care of those things. My wife has reached the point where she has decided she wants to do something else." When husbands do "pitch in" (a favorite phrase) it is likely to be at a task their wives tell them to do, so they still bear none of the responsibility for planning and preparing for what needs to be done. Or they'll take care of some once-in-a-while, out-of-the-ordinary project, like broiling a steak at an annual barbecue instead of cooking dinner every night—or even every other night.

The all-purpose and often acceptable excuse that workaholics offer to avert or answer all objections is that they're tired. Another advertising execu-

tive said, "You're very tired when you get home and
there's not much giving left." And who can argue?
After all, they were up working till 1 A.M. the night
before, and up-and-at-'em again at 5:00 that morning. But, as already mentioned, workaholics find the
time to do what they want to do, and they are
exhilarated—not exhausted—by work. So when they
say they "don't have time" or they're "too tired" they
really mean that they "don't want to."

The "I'm tired" strategy is not without its advantages for workaholics. As psychotherapist Maryanne
Vandervelde wrote in her recent book, *The Changing
Life of the Corporate Wife,* "A wife who accepts her
'proper' corporate role does, in reality, allow the
executive much more time and energy to devote to
climbing the corporate ladder. If you never have to
cook your own dinner, take your own shirts to the
laundry, arrange social engagements, hassle with the
cleaning lady, worry about the details of a move, or
stay home with a sick child, you can work harder,
longer, and more efficiently."

In *I Married a Bestseller,* Sheila Hailey's au-
tobiographical account of her life as the wife of Arthur Hailey, the workaholic author, she advises
would-be writers to "marry someone like me":

> A writer needs a person around who can cope; who
> can write letters, answer telephones, deal with
> plumbers and carpenters, discourage interruptions,
> and pay the bills. As friends have heard me mutter
> time and again: "Dammit! I do everything around
> here except write the books!"

Schedules and schedule conflicts are another source of conflict. Sheila Hailey continues, describing her adjustment to her husband's rigid schedule:

> Arthur is essentially a morning person, whereas I tend to be a night person. Over the years we have compromised—by my going to bed early and my getting up early.

Others mentioned waiting up for or being awakened by their workaholic spouses, who need so little sleep.

What may be most maddening is the sense of coming in second. Many wives mentioned feeling that their husbands cared more for their work than for them. Dr. Maurice Prout, assistant professor of mental health sciences and director of behavior therapies at Hahnemann Medical College in Philadelphia, maintains that "if you choose work for a lover, you'll have trouble with your wife." One woman spoke movingly of subjugating her desires to "a third member of our marriage known as 'the business.'" Her husband conceded that his eighty- to ninety-hour workweek and extensive travel once made her suspect he was working that way only to avoid her.

Some people suspect that their workaholic spouses are having affairs when they aren't. When workaholics do engage in extramarital sex, their work provides the perfect cover. But more often, I suspect, it is the workaholic's mate who may be seeing someone else. After all, who has more free time to fill?

So why would anyone ever marry a workaholic? Spouses usually knew what was in store: Workaholics were that way when they met. One woman told me she should have known what she was in for when her husband called his office the second day of their honeymoon. Others know what they're in for because they met at work. But even they often fail to realize that what may have been a distinct advantage in the office can be a disaster at home.

One couple I surveyed consisted of a male securities analyst who was a workaholic and a female secretary who was not. She commented that her workaholic mate cannot stop thinking or talking about business. He tends to turn their bedroom into a boardroom and their kitchen table into a conference table. "Sometimes," she concedes, "I just have to say, 'I don't want to hear it'—especially over Sunday breakfast or a candlelight dinner. He stops for a while, but the topic usually goes back to business later on."

Similarly, Beverly Holding met her husband Hal when both were working at a bookstore. She now works for the telephone company, while he has since become a publisher's rep. His position and territory necessitate spending many nights on the road and taking care of paperwork at home. Beverly said, "I love Hal, but I used to see more of him when we worked together."

Press accounts confirm that workaholism and marriage may not always mix. A 1976 *Princeton Alumni Weekly* profile of R. W. Apple, Jr., of *The New York Times,* contrasted his professional and personal lives:

Even on the run, he manages to organize his professional life with the skill of a radio program director, juggling interviews and flights, seeming to
be everywhere on days when there are primaries in
several states, and rarely missing a deadline.
Meanwhile, his private life falls into rampant dis-
organization, unpaid bills pile up at home, and his
house plants die. His marriage suffered from neglect to the point of a recent divorce.

Indeed, several workaholics I interviewed wondered why their spouses stuck with them or else
didn't blame them a bit in those cases where they had
not. One can't pin divorce on any single factor, but
every divorced workaholic I interviewed considered
work a contributory factor. In fact, an eminent
scientist said, "My first marriage was a failure on the
altar of workaholism." A man in the midtown-
Manhattan headquarters of what is probably the
world's most prestigious consulting firm finished
describing a typical day and paused to observe:

That puts a tremendous strain on your family. . . .
It takes a tremendous toll. You look at our New
York office and look at the married versus unmar-
ried and the divorce rate . . . is very high, and
high, in my opinion, among some of our best, best
people. I sincerely hope that I do not join their
ranks. There is no sign that I am now, but I . . .
look at myself realistically and say "I've got a fine,
solid marriage." But so did those guys.

Some people undoubtedly try to tell themselves
that a prospective spouse's workaholism is only a
temporary phenomenon, that the workaholic will
willingly change once he or she becomes better es-
tablished, settles down, gets older, becomes a part-

ner, and so on. Workaholics themselves sometimes
say the same things. Others probably think that they
can transform the workaholic. They're wrong.

Still others welcome a prospective spouse's
workaholism. One woman went so far as to openly
offer no objections to a workaholic mate. An ad I
clipped from the personal section of *The New Haven
Advocate* read as follows (italics mine):

(N53) **Warm, loving, extremely attractive,** educated
woman in early 30s would like to meet an unattached
educated professional man in his 40s. Looks not important. Capacity for loving, sharing and a sense of
humor are. *A "workaholic" would be okay.* I'm a
strictly one-man woman with no dependents, who enjoys her job, tennis, dining, theatre, reading, conversation, and will promise not to discuss mutual horo-
scope signs.

From *The New Haven Advocate*, August 2, 1978.

Dr. Jay Rohrlich, a Manhattan psychiatrist, suggests that spouses sometimes want the success,
status, and salary that workaholics tend to win without realizing that they'll be the ones to pay the price
for these prizes. Or they think that being married to a
workaholic will make it possible to retain and maintain much of the independence they enjoyed when
they were single. They're right.

A workaholic will be particularly appealing to a
fellow workaholic, since they have similar needs. Indeed, Dr. Prout finds that there are far fewer problems
when both partners are workaholics. "Strangely

enough, there's a good homeostasis there. . . . They have the work that will sustain them. There's no demand for intimacy. They have the same needs." That is, their expectations for themselves and for each other are essentially the same, so fights are few. They may not spend much time together but they can stay married to each other.

Why isn't home more important to workaholics?

Dr. Alexandra Symonds, a New York psychiatrist, feels that "some people require distance or power. They can't deal with intimacy." Upon reflection, she added that it might be easier to achieve a sense of intimacy, satisfaction, and control with work than with another person. "A lot of therapists are workaholics. I've heard of people who just schedule so many patients. It's like a substitute for a relationship. You can start it and stop it without its being sticky. And you get gratification, appreciation, and instant satisfaction. That's partly why doctors work so hard—you don't get that at home." Intimacy is incompatible with workaholism. "There is constant conflict of deciding 'Do I want to be at work?' versus 'Do I want to be with that person?'" explains Dr. Prout, the Philadelphia psychologist. Invariably, work wins.

Pity the people who want to come between them and their work. Workaholics have a rich inner life and a low need for intimacy. Aloof and alone, they are possibly incapable of sustaining intimate relationships. Brief encounters are enough, and superficial social contacts with colleagues and clients, business partners and prospects are far more comfortable than more intense involvements. What was particularly painful to see in the course of conducting these interviews was the disproportionate amounts of attention accorded to protégés and to progeny. Several male workaholics seemed more attached to, more available for, fonder of, and sometimes prouder of these "professional children"— students, subordinates, and such—than their actual children.

Life on the job is just more exciting than homelife. The people you encounter through work are—or at least seem to be—more exciting than those who share your more ordinary times. After all, they have the same professional interests and are always seen at their best. Family and friends can't hold a candle to them, so social life cannot compete. Dr. John Meeks, a psychiatrist who has treated the children of many Washington workaholics, told a reporter, "Home and kids seem dull when you've spent a day doing vital things like sweating on a hotline over whether a bomb will be dropped somewhere."

The question of which comes first—the workaholism or the isolation—is difficult to answer. It is possible that workaholics avoid friends and friendships because of the time they take. As a young, single man explained, "You get obligations to this person and that person that can really take your mind off what you want to be doing, which is your work." It is also plausible that workaholics are too self-involved and preoccupied to attract other people and too busy to sustain any relationships that start. Similarly, they may let professional involvements take precedence over and interfere with personal ones until friends or lovers lose interest.

The alternative possibility is that feeling "out of it"—that is, experiencing disappointments and a lack of success in the social sphere—leads people to commit themselves to school or work, where success and fulfillment are more easily attained or assured. This investment leads to increased involvement in work because opportunities to become more at ease socially are thus excluded. As these activities become even more fearsome and unfamiliar, the importance of work grows. This leads to increased isolation, too.

The lack of closeness and communication also comes into play in smaller ways, as well. Large segments of a workaholic's existence, from close associates to major projects and even trips, are not shared with a spouse—sometimes even a workaholic's daily whereabouts are unknown. There are simply too many things going on to keep track of them all. For instance, Alan Chodos, a Yale University physicist, complains that he cannot keep his wife's complicated schedule in his head. His wife, Dr. Florence Haseltine, is a Yale gynecologist whose day typically involves seeing patients, performing surgery, conducting research, teaching classes, and writing. As a result, Chodos explained, "even though she has a beeper, and even though she has an office, and even though there are about twelve different numbers at which she can be reached, there are times when it's hard to get hold of her."

Another man has the same problem. He recalled

a time when he and his wife were scheduled to take a
7 A.M. flight, but she still wasn't home at 1 A.M. the
night before. Wondering where she was, he tried calling her office, but the central switchboard had long
since shut down for the night. Worried, he got hold
of her building's night watchman and had him track
her down. The watchman found her hunched over
her desk, hard at work.

When only one person in a pair is a workaholic,
there is, according to Dr. Prout, "a sense of neglect
and a drifting apart." Recourse other than divorce
can take several forms. Spouses may retreat con-
structively (to do their own thing) or destructively
(to sulk and, perhaps, succumb to drugs and/or
drinking). Or they may try to compete either inside
the home or out as though to say, "I have no time for
you either."

On the other hand, the workaholic's demands
and schedule may create a very comfortable routine
for a spouse. One woman, for example, is starting to
explore employment possibilities now that all of her
children are in school all day. However, her search
seems half-hearted. Perhaps there is more status in
being "Mrs. Successful Management Consultant"
than in being something with less status in her own
right. Perhaps she would hate to give up the opportunity to travel with her husband when glamorous
business trips come his way. And perhaps it is reas-
suring to tell herself she's needed at home and
couldn't take a demanding job herself since she certainly couldn't work late. After all, someone has to

be home for the children. So, all in all, she may have put up with a lot—but may have realized the security of certain benefits and the safety of certain limits in return. In other words, his work has defined what and how much she could do.

Lady Bird Johnson once said that all politicians should be orphans and bachelors. Her prescription is equally plausible for workaholics in other professions. Nancy Hardin, a vice president of Paramount Pictures, would probably agree. She told *Working Woman:*

> I can't imagine what my life would have been like if I had had children. I see people combining careers and motherhood, but usually they have husbands and nannies—a lot of help. There's never a moment when I feel I shouldn't be working. . . . I go out a lot at night to see friends or go to screenings. I sandwich in the work, getting up an hour early to read a script or the trade papers, and I read some more after I come home at night. But you can't manage it all when you're living with someone. You can be sure he'll take it personally.

Time and timing conspire against the workaholic who is also a parent. The hours of work—including a time-consuming commute at each end—in conjunction with the "life crunch," in which people in their 20s and 30s may be establishing families and careers simultaneously, don't leave much time for establishing a loving tie with children. One woman workaholic in her 30s explained that, while she can readily squeeze in paperwork between the hours of 1 A.M. and 4 A.M., she cannot spend time with her small son then.

What happens to the children of workaholics? Dr. Prout told a reporter that "children in a marriage dominated by commitment to work usually turn out one of two ways: Either they are carbon copies, intense and hard-driving, or else they are exact opposites, beach bums or the equivalent."

Workaholic parents usually don't want their children to follow in their footsteps. One woman who did anyway has come to share her father's disdain for those who don't work as hard as she does: "I have a tremendous contempt for men who don't work hard, but I also don't want to be involved with a workaholic because I don't want to live that kind of life."

Her brother, now in his late 20s, comments, "My father was much better at economic support than at emotional support." He described the series of responses that characterized his relationship with his father. First, resentment: "I used to hate it because he was never around." Second, rebellion: "I dropped out of school and went through a number of schools." Third, gratitude: "Seeing him work hard and succeed made me feel I could succeed, too, if I worked hard."

Their father's work ethic has been a double-edged sword for them and their three siblings. On one hand, according to the daughter, "all of us are the beneficiaries of my father's hard work and his largess because we've had opportunities that other people whose fathers sat in front of TV with a beer can didn't have." On the other hand, she and at least several of her brothers and sisters have undergone therapy. "My mother once said that if my father had gone, maybe all of us wouldn't have had to go."

Several fathers seemed unwilling or unable to face these facts. They don't know and don't want to know where they stand. I requested that the questionnaires I mailed out to workaholics be distributed also to people at home or at work. Manhattan management consultant Lester Buck (not his real name) balked when his wife suggested giving one to their teenaged son. Les barked, "I don't want to give him one." His wife suspects that her husband was terrified that he would find out just how his son feels about the situation. Similarly, an ad executive claimed that there was no conflict between his personal and professional lives, but he nonetheless conceded that his daughter jokes about "that man who comes around here once in a while," in reference to his long hours and heavy travel load.

Indeed, some children are very much aware of a missing parent. Helen, aged 10, is one of the case studies included in *Privileged Ones,* an account of children from affluent families researched and written by Robert Coles, a Harvard psychiatrist. Her situation is poignant:

> There's only one reason I like to go to our country house—because Daddy is there. All week we don't see much of him. Sometimes I'm lucky if I see him for five minutes in the morning before I go to

school. . . . And a lot of times he doesn't get
home before we go to bed. I miss him. So does my
brother, Geoff. He says he wishes Daddy would
lose his job, then we'd have him here at home.
Geoff says he even *prays* that Daddy will lose his
job.

Coles explains that when this father takes time off
from his Boston business to be with his children,
"they ask him, right off, how long it will be until he
leaves. They also ask him when they will *next* see
him." In a school essay Helen expanded upon her
predicament:

My Daddy is going to be president of his company
one of these days. I heard him tell my mother that.
He said he had to work day and night, but in the
end it would be worth it. My mother is not so sure.
My brother, Geoff, and I are not sure, either. My
brother and I wish our father could be home with
us, and not at the office or traveling all day and
half the night. . . . but it is because Daddy has
such a good job that we can have all the toys and
live where we do. You can't have everything. Our
mother tells us that. I know what she means.

Children are well aware of the other parent's
reactions. One woman, now grown, recalls that it
was understood and unquestioned that her father
would work all day Saturdays and half of Sundays.
What she remembers most about these weekends is
that when it was time for her father to go to work on
Sunday, her mother would always cry.

Even young children learn early on to consult
the calendar to see if a workaholic parent will be

available. Some even ask for "appointments" with their parents. But children tire of conforming to the workaholic's plans and schedules. Lester Buck's son contends that "the only way to spend time with Daddy is to go to the hardware store and the dry cleaner [on weekend errands] and that's no fun." He has developed a desperate trick to get some of his father's time and attention: He'll deny having any homework when his mother asks him, only to show it to his father the second he walks in the door. He knows that "the only thing his father will do is help with homework."

Children typically see only the sad side of workaholism. They see their fathers or mothers not when they are at work and enjoying it, but when they are at home, bushed, beat, and bored or reading the paper. Many children of work addicts become convinced that Mommy or Daddy would rather be reading *The Wall Street Journal* than spending time with them.

They may well be right. When workaholic parents do spend time with their children, they are more apt to be driven by duty than by desire. Thus, the so-called "quality" of time suffers as much as the "quantity." Some mothers and fathers "forget" how little time they manage to spend with their children; the children do not. Parents can never make it up. Many workaholics sincerely expect to spend more time with their children "someday." But by then, children are apt to be grown and out on their own. One man reminisced that his workaholic father had suddenly shown up on campus one weekday when he was a college sophomore. The son, surprised, asked, "What are you doing here?" His father answered, "I want to spend time with you." His son had to tell him, "It's too late."

6
Workaholics:
At "Play"

*They are never less at leisure than when
they are at leisure.*
—William H. Whyte

"Workaholics at play" is almost a contradiction
in terms, for work addicts have a difficult time enjoying themselves in almost any leisure-time activity,
from sports and hobbies to vacations and even sex.
In fact, most workaholics are unable—not just
unwilling—to get away from it all. Time off doesn't
tempt them. Weekends are unwelcome interruptions
of the workday week. And summers, when everyone
else slows down, leaves early, and takes vacations,
are particularly exasperating.

Because it is less structured than work, leisure
time leaves workaholics at a loss for what to do.
Eileen Ford, the head of the world-famous modeling
agency, observes, "When I work less, I become restless." Workaholics practically climb the walls when
they can't work. Even short periods of inactivity are

intolerable; workaholics literally can't sit still and do nothing. They feel guilty unless they're doing something productive, or at least constructive, such as reading professionally relevant literature. This inability to relax, even at home, is part of what turns their houses into branch offices of their businesses.

Even rest and sleep are suspect. Their motto might as well be, "If you snooze, you lose." Few, of course, have had a better chance to test this hypothesis than Jimmy Carter. As James Wooten reported in *Dasher*, when Carter was in the midst of his two-year campaign to capture the presidency, his family begged him to slow down a bit. He told them:

> I can will myself to sleep until ten-thirty and get my ass beat, or I can will myself to get up at six o'clock and become the President of the United States.

The reluctance to rest is probably due to an overabundance of energy. One publisher complained, "I can't calm down; I can't come down." A public relations representative explained, "I have too much energy." After every twelve-hour working day, she would walk across the street to work out at a gym to use up some of the excess. (She was not engaging in mild calisthenics either, but in strenuous gymnastics.)

Their stamina sets them apart. It far exceeds that of other people, and this poses some problems. One surgeon has long made a practice of waking at 5:00 A.M. and doing his first operation at 7:00. He finds, however, that "people are immediately judging you by their own standards of stamina. I sleep a maximum of five hours—I don't really need anymore—but I leave parties early so nobody gets nervous."

Any thought of rest or relaxation frightens workaholics because leisure looks a lot like the laziness they loathe. Workaholics will back off from it until it becomes so foreign and unfamiliar that they "forget" how to do it. One esteemed economist concedes she has worked so hard for so long that she has "forgotten how to relax." She, like many, feels this is "something I can relearn someday." However, its unlikely that she'll want to, and even if she does, it's even less likely that she'll be able to.

When inactivity is inescapable, workaholics react in one of two ways. Some go to ridiculous lengths to go about their business. Snowbound executives, for example, have resorted to strapping on cross-country skis to get to their offices. Coronary victims have had telephones installed by their beds in the intensive care units. David Halberstam reportedly described Fred Silverman, the TV executive, as someone who "would make sure the previous day's Neilsens would be delivered to him by bicycle rider" if he were visiting China. No wonder Japan Air Lines offers an "Executive Service Lounge" in a Tokyo hotel and advertises it as "your office away from the office."

At the other extreme, a few retreat. Dr. Nelson Bradley, a Chicago psychiatrist, has found that "if the work addict is forced into inactivity, he may shut off the world, lying around doing absolutely nothing."[1] Sally MacKinnon, a marketing executive with R. J. Reynolds Tobacco Company in North Carolina, remarks that sometimes she doesn't budge during an entire weekend. Despite being on-the-go all week, she finds that on Saturdays and Sundays she has "the metabolism of a garden slug."

Some workaholics do allow themselves certain leisure activities as long as these directly benefit their work. For instance, taking time to jog at 5 P.M. is tolerable because you can return refreshed, restored, and ready to work several hours longer. Louis L'Amour, author of almost eighty historical novels about the American West, manages to make some aspects of his work more like other people's play by scouting locations that will serve as settings for his western novels. He told *Los Angeles Magazine*, "I like to hike in the mountains, I like to explore. I like to come into the back country, and I can do it because it's part of my business."

When workaholics make a conscious effort to take time off, you can be sure that they work hard to have fun. Indeed, for many work addicts, the leisure pursuits that everyone else seems to enjoy soon become just a different kind of job. One workaholic told his therapist that "fun" was something you learned to have by working hard at it. Just as workaholics turn their work into play, so too do they turn their play into work.

Even sex becomes just another task to cross off on the "things to do" list. Some people have conjectured that workaholics work so hard because they are sublimating their unsuccessful or deviant sexual drives. But noted sex researchers and therapists William Masters and Virginia Johnson consider sexual difficulties more as a consequence of work addiction, not a cause. They wrote that sexuality is "profoundly affected . . . by conscious and/or unconscious feelings that are rooted in attitudes about work. . . . Victims of a distorted work ethic generally manifest one or two major misconceptions about the nature of sexual response. Either they exalt work to the highest priority in their lives and relegate sex to the lowest, or they approach their sex in fundamentally the same fashion as they do their work."[2] Some may try to beat the national average of sexual activity instead of simply enjoying it for its own sake. Others, guilty because they're not working, are liable to become sexually crippled or repressed. Otherwise, they tend to be structured, scheduled, or rigid—writing in "sex" on their calendars, for instance, as though it were a chore to finish as quickly as possible. Therefore, sex may not serve as a form of relaxation, recreation, or release for workaholics. "It is," explains psychiatrist Lawrence Susser, "a performance, and they feel they have to please their partners first."

There are also those people who use work as an excuse to avoid sexual encounters. They may fear that their "performance" will not measure up. Compounding this is the problem of boredom. Boredom may stem from comparing their spouses with the more "exciting" people encountered at work. Alter-

natively, it may mask anger at or disappointment
with their spouse, or boredom may just mean that
workaholics find monogamy, well, monotonous.

An example of this is Alan Jacobs (a
pseudonym) who owns and operates a cheese shop
in an exclusive New York City neighborhood and
endures a lengthy commute on the legendary Long
Island Railroad. Only 30, he looks, seems, and
sounds at least twenty years older. Workaholism, he
explains, is "not good for your sex life. You put so
many hours in, and truthfully, by the time you come
home, your libido is kind of worked out. I find that
being in the shop here and dealing with so many
absolutely gorgeous girls—they're like starlets,
young models, absolute dolls—and then you come
home to your wife . . . my wife's a doll, but she's a
'Plain Jane' sort of girl, and you're so tired and everything. It's murder on your sex life." The irony is that
his wife may think he's God's gift and wonder what's
wrong with her. His customers, on the other hand,
are unlikely to give him the time of day.

Some people talk of a new trend: Besides
homosexuality, and bisexuality, now there's talk of
what some have called the New Celibacy—
asexuality. One practitioner told the *Village Voice* in
1978, "To me, an asexual is someone who has no
desire for sex. Whether he repressed the desire is
something else. It's peculiar to people who are involved in their work and can't put all their energy
into too many sources." Significant scientific journals substantiate this. Articles have documented inhibited sexual desire and have, for the first time, fo-

cused on sexual inactivity rather than activity. Lack of sexual interest, however, may stem from and be compounded by workaholics' avoidance of intimacy. Dr. Helen Singer Kaplan, who heads the human sexuality program at New York Hospital–Cornell Medical Center, told *The New York Times Magazine* that "in our society, intimacy is more frightening than sex." And this, as we saw, in the last chapter, is doubly true for workaholics.

The characteristic of working hard to have fun is readily apparent in other parts of the workaholic's life, including hobbies and vacations. The father of a friend of mine was a cosmetic chemist in charge of developing complex compounds. For relaxation he took up carpentry. When he wanted to construct a louvered door, he wouldn't buy a pre-cut one. Instead, he sawed and sanded each louver *by hand.*

Similarly, one management consultant described a break in a business trip as follows: "We went out to Yosemite on the weekend and I think I just about drove my wife crazy. We went on what I think she would describe as a forced march as opposed to a walk in the woods." More than one workaholic's wife has been known to say, "I need a vacation from his vacation."

Since vacations can be so hard to take, many workaholics don't take them at all. A young copywriter had already accumulated more than a month of unused time. "Right now," she said, "I have five weeks of vacation and I don't know when I'm going to take it." Other work addicts merely take much less time than they are entitled to. An airline executive I

interviewed was eligible for unlimited vacation time
and unlimited first-class airfare for himself and his
family. Nonetheless, they had taken a total of two
five-day trips throughout the preceding year.

"A holiday or vacation," reports a 1974 *Fortune*
article, "is not so much a welcome respite as it is a
boring pause to be endured." In 1978, the president
of a Pennsylvania utility company told *The
Philadelphia Bulletin,* "I take my vacation in days
. . . I can't remember when I last took a couple of
weeks off at one time. . . . And even when I'm
away, I'm constantly available to my office." When
they do get away, they can hardly stay away. Almost
all call in and will, when work warrants, cut their
vacations short. One publisher has never taken the
full two weeks she schedules because, "by the third
day, I'm wondering what's on my desk."

One writer quips that "when workaholics go on
vacation, it is not the natives but the tourists who are
restless." One surgeon decided to try a vacation in
Mexico, but after only two days of sightseeing he
offered his services to a local hospital. Similarly,
Selma Field, who with her husband operates a public relations firm in upstate New York, described
their infrequent attempts at taking vacations: "Once
we won an all-expense paid two-week trip to Europe.
I think we lasted six days."[3]

Other people add on vacation days to a business trip, but not workaholics. One woman suspects
that her workaholic father stays trim strictly by
"running from airport to airport." She reports that
once, when he was with a client on the Greek island

From *The New York Times*, November 7, 1976. Copyright © 1976 by The New York Times Company. Reprinted by permission.

of Mykonos, the client had to shut down the airport to keep her father from leaving.

The willingness of workaholics to cut short their vacations affects other people as well. Workaholics will not hesitate to interrupt a subordinate's vacation (or honeymoon) if there is work to be done. While I was in the office of a Park Avenue law partner, I overheard him instruct his secretary to call an associate. "Get Dan," he said. "He's at the Hotel Meridien in Martinique." It also affects their families. Even on vacation, spouses cannot count on seeing much of workaholics. Nancy Kissinger recently told *Vogue* about an upcoming annual trip to Acapulco. "It's always a working vacation for Henry," she said. "We've never had the other kind."

Such working vacations might as well be taken separately. For example, Yale professors Alan Chodos and Florence Haseltine tend to skip each other's professional conferences. Chodos says, "She would go crazy at a conference of physicists because she would go crazy having nothing to do. Conversely, since most of her colleagues are men, it would just be me and the gynecologists' wives. There's nothing wrong with gynecologists' wives. I have nothing against them. It's just that I don't want to spend a week lying on the beach with them." He would ordinarily take more vacation trips than his wife would or could. But while Chodos can take the summer off or cart his books and papers anywhere, Haseltine's work requires her to be near her patients, hospital, and lab.

The only way that most workaholics can survive vacations is by combining their work and play. "Even on vacation, I have my typewriter, Xerox machine, telecopier, and four telephone lines with me," explained Dr. Elizabeth Whelan, author of numerous books and articles. She recently converted one floor of her vacation home into an office to accommodate all of this. As Stanley Marcus, chairman emeritus of Dallas' Neiman-Marcus department stores, wrote in his autobiography, *Minding the Store:*

> Vacations unadulterated by any business considerations have always been difficult for me to take, for there is hardly a place in the world that doesn't offer some buying or business opportunities or obligations.

Others, inadvertently, revert to work. Jeno Paulucci, founder of Chun King and other food companies, responded to my questionnaire while on vacation. He explained:

> I am now dictating this from Acapulco. Hell, I
> don't even leave the phone. I'm pacing around this
> pool, wondering what I should do next. I'm writing
> memos, calling the office, calling New York, calling
> Chicago. I just can't relax.

Some workaholics are manic about missing calls: They install answering machines with remote call-in features, or they hire answering services and check in constantly. One television reporter was so worried that he attached an answering machine to his unlisted telephone number *and* hired an answering service, just in case the machine broke.

There are a number of reasons why workaholics can't really accept vacations or time off. First of all, they haven't given vacations a fair trial. The short jaunts they take may be simultaneously too long to endure and too short to enjoy. Expecting too much from too little, they may remain itchy and return home before they've had a chance to unwind. Or they've tried the wrong type of vacation. They've taken the kind that is soothing—for instance, lying on a sandy beach—when what they would have preferred is the sort that is stimulating, such as experiencing an entirely new culture.

Second, they so enjoy what they do that they feel no need to "get away from it all." Their jobs resemble a long vacation. Many feel no need for any leisure time activities for much the same reason. According to *Newsweek*, Margaret Mead was astounded when a reporter once asked if her life wasn't a little bit dull without hobbies. "Why should I need any?" she exclaimed. "Anthropology is connected with the whole of life . . . with everything people do."

What they do for a living is simply more pleasurable than and preferable to any leisure pursuit that workaholics know. Consumer advocate Ralph Nader raised the rhetorical question of why watching a movie or a football game or listening to music is supposed to be so much more pleasurable than protecting the consumer interest. Having reversed the traditional pattern, they approach time off with feelings that are, at best, mixed. A partner in a prestigious investment bank admitted, "Sure, I'm looking forward to going skiing next week but not totally looking forward to going away. . . . We had a super day today. . . . Supposing next Friday is like that. I'd really kick myself for not being here."

Traditional forms of recreation seem like a waste of time and are quite incomprehensible to workaholics. When one of Nader's associates said he had spent the weekend lying on the beach, going on walks, and reading the newspapers, Nader responded in disbelief, "That takes all weekend?"[4] Then, too, their work may include ample opportunities for travel. Although Nader never takes vacations, he travels extensively, giving lectures. "The working trips," according to his biographer, Hays Gorey, "are vacations because Nader could not abide sitting on a beach somewhere, and the change of scenery does as much for him as a rest."

A lot of workaholics feel that the preparation and anxiety that precede taking time off are more trouble than they're worth. Workaholics work extra hard before they leave in order to get ahead, and they make elaborate precautions to ensure that the work will proceed in their absence. Sally MacKinnon never went away without leaving elaborate memos and detailed instructions for her staff. Once she did not, however, and was "amazed" to find that "things didn't fall apart."

Finally, workaholics want to remain on top of things and in complete control of their jobs. Since their jobs matter so much to them, they are somewhat afraid to go away and lose that control. As *Fortune* explains:

> His colleagues may use his absence to commit all manner of office atrocities—stealing his secretary, unfairly pinning the blame on him for someone else's error, reorganizing him out of his job, or even moving corporate headquarters. . . . proximity to one's interests is power; distance is impotence.

The inability of workaholics to enjoy vacations and avocations is a subject of concern to mental health professionals. When consulted by workaholics, counselors try to overcome these attitudes. Dr. Lawrence Susser, a psychiatrist who also trained as a pediatrician, believes that everyone—but especially the workaholic—must have a sense of balance with regard to work and play. He says, "Workaholics commit slow suicide by refusing to allow the child inside them to play." Dr. Susser likens the workaholics' distaste for leisure to children's claims that they hate spinach when they've never tasted it. Workaholic adults, he contends, haven't really given leisure a chance. He recommends returning to the pastimes that were pleasurable during childhood and adolescence. In both his private practice and his programs at professional conferences, he emphasizes rechanneling energy away from work.

Dr. Susser defines the workaholic in terms of transactional analysis. Workaholics, he explains, "are dominated by their controlling parent. . . . the adult is blocked . . . the natural child is also blocked and that's the key to the therapy." In contrast to other mental health practitioners, Susser does not practice the traditional passive therapeutic process. He maintains that "talking to a workaholic in my early experience was fruitless and painful for me as a therapist. You don't get anywhere talking to them. They stay obstructive and you get gray hair and headaches. . . . To me, playing is a natural way of life. I took it for granted. It comes easily to me. My intuitive solution was to get these people outdoors and it worked."

Susser's outdoor play therapy starts with a six- to eight-hour hike ("I bring my dog along; that usually brings out the child in them") that includes a two-hour lunch. "Have you ever seen a workaholic take two hours for lunch?" said Susser. "After half an hour, they begin to get restless. There's a voice inside them that says 'Shouldn't you start to clean up?' "

Dr. Jay Rohrlich, a Manhattan psychiatrist, often prescribes vacations during the course of psychotherapy and considers it "a sign of progress" when workaholic patients take them. But there's some danger that the cure will just worsen the condition. Suzanne Corry, a leisure counselor, cautions converts not to demand too much from themselves and not to drive themselves to become experts when they initiate leisure activities. Corry told *The Philadelphia Inquirer* reporter, Darrell Sifford, "You can enjoy a walk in the woods without trying to learn the names of the trees and the bugs."

7
Workaholics:
Are They Happy?

*I really have so much fun I ought to be
arrested.*
—I. F. Stone

The old idea that all workaholics are frustrated,
harried, tired, and unhappy simply is not true. In
fact, as a group, the workaholics I interviewed were
remarkably satisfied and content with their lives.
Stan Michaels (not his real name) is a good example.
Stan is in his late 30s and lives in a well-to-do suburb
of New York with his wife and their young children.
He has been in advertising for about ten years, but
doesn't seem fazed by the alleged perils of his pro-
fession. "Friends say, 'Gee, I hear advertisers have
ulcers. . . . They have problems, pressures, and
people get fired.' I see it, but I don't feel it."

His face is bright, his energy apparent, and his
enthusiasm for his work is obvious. "The thing that's
so fascinating about advertising is that you study a

lot of other businesses," he explains, "It's never boring. Every day seems only six hours long."

Photographs of his family fill his office. He devotes considerable time on the weekends to them, explaining, "Our social life is built around the kids. My idea of a Saturday night is to go out with the kids and another family that has kids." However, as he freely admits, "By Sunday I want to get back to work."

Michaels acknowledges his workaholism without apologies or regrets. He says, "I don't feel I'm missing anything. I think I do more. . . . I really don't feel I have the problems that you should have if you're a workaholic."

However, there were those like Hank Schulz (a pseudonym) who clearly paid a price for their work addiction. Schulz is in his mid-40s and lives and works in New Jersey. He has never been married. Schulz has spent the last twenty years with the same publishing firm. He was recently demoted from a senior position in the firm's San Francisco headquarters. He attributes his lack of success there to a tendency to try to do everything himself, which antagonized others. He went through four secretaries in the last two years.

He is less than satisfied with his present sales position. "I think the unfortunate thing in my business is that I operate totally at the convenience of other people. . . . I call on accounts and [their] customers come in and it takes three hours to do something that can be done in a half hour."

Cognizant of the consequences of his work habits, he describes his social life as minimal. "I haven't seen friends. I've driven people away." Puffing on a cigarette, he complains about his health. "I haven't had a check-up since 1975. I've put on weight and haven't had any decent exercise." He freely admits that he is a workaholic, which he defines as "somebody who overworks, who does the work and a little bit more . . . who probably does it more than it should be done, who probably does too much of it without letting other people do anything, and who would rather come in on a Saturday than do anything else."

Others expressed regret over divorce, over time lost with their children, over promotions that didn't come at work. Women workaholics seem to have a particularly difficult time. Although the motivations behind and manifestations of workaholism are essentially the same for either sex, what can and does differ are the consequences for men and women.

Dr. Alexandra Symonds, associate clinical professor of psychiatry at New York University School of Medicine and a member of the faculty of the Karen Horney Institute, thinks that "in an indirect way, workaholism might make a man more attractive to women." The reverse—that women's workaholism makes them more attractive to men—is unlikely to be true: "At this point," explains Dr. Symonds, "men might be threatened by it." Although the gap is closing, the personal, social, and sexual penalties that workaholism may impose still seem to be more pro-

nounced for women than for men. Men are more apt
to find women willing to come in second to a job or a
schedule.

The man in a woman workaholic's life may
think she doesn't need him or that her work is more
important to her. (Or, as a colleague of mine concluded crudely, "Women workaholics would rather get
paid than laid.") Cathy Guisewhite, the 28-year-old
single cartoonist behind the comic strip "Cathy,"
which portrays the perils of a modern-day un-
married Pauline, told a *Washington Post* reporter, "I
really throw myself into what I do. That's probably
my greatest asset. My work becomes my entertainment. . . . part of my personal problem is that my
main lover is my work." The suspicion that women
workaholics are possibly sexless, certainly dateless,
and (if married) more likely than most to wind up in
divorce court is baseless. But a woman workaholic *is*
likely to encounter more difficulties in finding and
keeping a mate than her male counterpart.

While a male workaholic might *want* a woman
who does not work as hard as he does and is therefore available to cater to his needs, his female counterpart is much less likely to respect a man who
doesn't work hard, too. She needs someone who is
equally involved in an endeavor of his own. Such a
man must keep up—in terms of energy, intellect, and,
in many cases, income. One woman's marriage broke
up, in part, because her husband minded her making
more money than he did. She referred to her divorce
as "the dues women have to pay."

A woman workaholic has to cope with a special

set of concerns. She may feel pressure to conform to the stereotypical role and do double duty—working all day and going home to a "second job" at night. If she succumbs to the domestic drudgery, she may be exhausted. If she doesn't succumb, she may be embarrassed and guilty.

Anyone who still expects or wants a woman to be frivolous and flighty instead of practical and organized will be sorely disappointed by a woman workaholic. The boyfriend of one woman I interviewed asked her what she wanted for Christmas and was taken aback when she answered, "A filing cabinet." Similarly, the husband of an insurance agent was absolutely astounded when he saw that in her appointment book, she had pencilled in time for sex with him.

These seeming differences may mean it's tougher for a woman to be a workaholic or they may just be the result of the spotlight placed on women who work and the microscopic analysis of their every action and attitude. One accomplished single woman bristled when asked how her personal and professional lives conflicted. She angrily asserted, "You rarely find, when a man is interviewed, that people say, 'What about your social life?' You never ask a guy who's in a pressured position—be he 20 years old or 70—'Do you have time for your family? Do you have time to be a daddy to your kids? Do you have time to go out on dates?'"

And indeed, screenwriter Paul Brody (a pseudonym), indicates that the differences between men and women workaholics may be diminishing in the social-sexual sphere, too. He said, "Being a workaholic means a social life can be kind of difficult because women feel threatened and competitive. When they're with you, they don't want to share you. . . . I get very impatient with women who are making demands on me I don't think I can meet, who ultimately have no lives of their own. Maybe it's naive of me to think you can have a love affair with work and a love affair with a woman. What I would like to seek are women who are involved in their own thing . . . and not looking to me to define them."

But one inescapable difference undoubtedly remains. Concerns about bearing and caring for children do distinguish women workaholics—and all working women, in general—from their male counterparts. Dr. Elizabeth Whelan, whose books include *A Baby? . . . Maybe: A Guide to Making the Most Fateful Decision of Your Life,* had her first child in 1977 and hired full-time help. She finds, "Sometimes I simply cannot understand how anyone could have a second child. I am exhausted. But sometimes I also feel it might be worth it to accept the challenge."

Jay Rohrlich, a Manhattan psychiatrist, has observed a tendency for workaholic women to postpone parenthood and opt out of it entirely. While it may well be that they are consciously concentrating on making their careers and cognizant that they don't have the time that parenting takes, there's more to it than that. Dr. Rohrlich suspects that many are perfectionists, who are accustomed to accomplishing, achieving, excelling, and who assume—quite correctly—that "it's far easier to have a perfect career than a perfect child."

So women workaholics seem to face special problems. But in the end I found that there was very little difference between men and women workaholics in what made them happy and what made them frustrated. My research showed that there were four basic issues.

The most important was homelife. The more a spouse and children accepted the fact of the workaholic's addiction and accommodated to the situation, the better the chance of fulfillment for the workaholic—and for the marriage. But the really crucial factor here was whether the workaholic felt free of the responsibility for supervising or performing household duties. It wasn't just who goes for the groceries, but who makes the shopping list and who feels guilty when the cats—or the kids—have nothing to eat. Even nonessential domestic responsibilities intrude upon workers' lives and interfere with their work.

The second strongest determinant of fulfillment was how much autonomy and variety they had in their work. The more control and novelty in their jobs, the happier they were.

Third, the more closely the skills and personal styles of the workaholics matched the demands of their jobs, the happier they were. There seemed to be two ways of achieving this congruence. The first one was to find the right career and the right job: As a magazine editor explained, "There is no question that I have found my spot." The second was to analyze their strengths and weaknesses and find the best way to make a significant contribution: As a restaurateur admitted, "I limit my activities to those areas where I'm able to be unique, or at least very good."

The fourth issue was health; the better workaholics feel, the more fulfilled they are. (However, it was hard to get a handle on the true importance of health; as a group, my subjects were extremely healthy.) It was interesting to note that actual ailments can be much less immobilizing or intrusive than imagined illnesses. One man, for example, once went from the operating room to his office in under six hours (to his doctor's disbelief); on the other hand, the slightest symptom would send another man straight to his physician's office.

However, when workaholics *do* get sick, they make particularly poor patients. Restrictions enrage them. One woman said that she was sure her husband would survive his heart attack, but she was less sure that he could survive the required recuperation period.

Some workaholics, it seems, value work more highly than life itself. In 1956, noted sex researcher Alfred Kinsey received a stern warning from his doctor to stop working so hard. Kinsey, who had already suffered several heart attacks, was told he could live for two more years if he would work only four hours a day. Kinsey reportedly told a friend that if he couldn't work, he didn't want to live. He continued working his typical long hours and died two months later.[1]

Although homelife and health are important to work addicts, the bottom line is that if they're happy with their jobs, chances are they'll be satisfied elsewhere. As one woman explained, "If I'm happy with work, I'm very happy at home." Workaholics admit, albeit reluctantly, that job satisfaction simply matters more to them. An attorney concluded that the role of job satisfaction in his total life satisfaction was "more than I'd like to admit." When I asked an eminent scientist about the role of work relative to other sources of satisfaction, he said, "Oh, that's all of it. It's my real satisfaction."

The importance of work seems to hold for the whole working population. Jane Brody reported in *The New York Times* that "job satisfaction is surpassed only by love and marriage as being important to happiness. In one study, 70 percent of the people who were happy in their jobs were also happy with life generally, but only 14 percent of those unhappy with their jobs said they were happy. The factors that affect job satisfaction include interest in and value of the work, income, security, chance for advancement, flexible hours, and vacation time." And the 1973 H.E.W. study, *Work in America,* reported that job satisfaction was highly predictive of longevity. In other words, people who like their jobs live longer than those who don't.

Workaholics would add that the longer you work, the longer you live. Workaholics of all ages worry about what would happen if they were to work less. They can grow quite alarmed at the mere thought of slowing down. There is some question as to whether trying to change is advisable, since doing so is apt to be stressful in itself. There is also the question of whether such a change is feasible. Now that he's in his late 50s, Shelly Gross regrets that he lacks the financial freedom to give it all up, sit back and enjoy life. Of course, as he concedes, "a lot of people say I couldn't sit back." One of these is undoubtedly his wife, Joan, a psychiatric social worker. "She says I wear her out."

Some are simply afraid of stopping. Despite her advancing age, Giuliana di Camerino still works almost twenty hours a day supervising her international group of stores, known as Roberta di Camerino. She told an interviewer, "It is not clever to work so much . . . I am ashamed at my age. . . . Work is one of the secrets to remaining young. . . . The day you stop, you become an old woman."[2]

What accounts for this reluctance to retire? A team of social scientists at Iowa State University reviewed the research literature linking both job satisfaction and work commitment to negative attitudes toward retirement. They then found support for the link in their own study of 2,000 employed men, aged 50 and over. Their results, published in the Journal of Gerontology, may be somewhat exaggerated because of the ages of the members of their sample.[3] As the *Journal of Occupational Psychology* reported in 1976, there often exists an inverse relationship between the proximity of retirement and its attractiveness. However, in my own research, workaholics as young as 35 were apt to remark, as one did, "I want to die when they hand me the watch. Retirement to me is the most dreadful thought in the world."

For some, the supposed social reform of enforced retirement is as repressive as the enforced labor it supplanted. The American Medical Association has issued a statement opposing forced retirement, which reads in part:

> The physical and mental health of an individual can be affected by loss of status, lack of meaningful activity, fear of becoming dependent, and by isolation. Compulsory retirement produces a chain reaction in the health of such persons. Man's increasing life expectancy will prove of little use to him if at an arbitrary age, he is denied the right to work and produce.[4]

A later statement, also issued by the A.M.A., said:

> The sudden cessation of productive work and earning power of an individual caused by compulsory retirement at the chronological age of 65, often leads to physical and emotional deterioration and premature death.[5]

The recent controversy concerning the age of mandatory retirement made no difference at all to most workaholics. They either planned to work or were already working beyond either 65 or 70, although they had absolutely no financial need to do so. William Batten, for instance, had to step down from the top spot at J. C. Penney, in 1974, when he reached 65. He immediately immersed himself in directorships and ultimately returned to full-time work as chairman of the New York Stock Exchange. He told a *New York Times* reporter: "If I could think of many more ways to have fun than working, I would stop working and do that."

Prominent workaholics, in particular, face the unpleasant transition from *Who's Who* to "Who's that?" As Dr. Harry Levinson, a psychological consultant, wrote in *Psychological Man*, "The anticipated crises for a person approaching retirement has chiefly to do with loss of contact with the organization, loss of purpose, and the feeling of being totally forgotten and having little value to others." Workaholics typically postpone retiring as long as possible, retire reluctantly if they must, and often return to work even then. But the second career often amounts to only a carbon copy of the first. Richard S. Salant reached the mandatory retirement age (65) at C.B.S. and started work the next day as vice chairman of N.B.C., a C.B.S. arch rival. Described by a colleague as "a workaholic who is 65 going on 36," Salant conceded in an interview with *The New York Times*, "I'm terrified of retirement. A few months ago, I told anyone who asked that I would probably teach at Columbia and write a book. But the truth is, I don't know how to teach or how to write a book."

Thus, the fear that workaholics shorten their lives through stress may be unfounded. Stress is not necessarily bad. While it may cause heart attacks in some people, it's what makes workaholics tick. The difference between coping with and collapsing from stress depends on the body's response to it. Individual people can be compared to the strings of a violin: Each one requires a different degree of tautness or tension. Suzanne C. Kobasa, a University of Chicago psychologist, studied executives at a midwestern utility and found that only 20 percent of those under high stress got sick. The majority weathered the storm in perfect health. The healthy ones, says Kobasa, shared three characteristics: the belief that they can control or influence the events in their jobs; an ability to feel deeply involved in or committed to the activities of their lives; and the anticipation of change as an exciting challenge to further development.[6]

In fact, insufficient stress may lead to more sickness. One study of 1,540 bank officers found that people experiencing too little stress show as high an incidence of stress-related disease as those experiencing too much. In other words, those who, like workaholics, need stimulation can literally be bored to death.[7]

There is, however, some danger that workaholics fail to recognize their limits or realize the stress that they do face. As one workaholic told me, a bit defensively, "What's to say that having such a full life and doing all this stuff is wrong? . . . I don't seem the least bit tired." But one authority has claimed that such an energetic manner may mask chronic fatigue.

Workaholics will experience strain, Dr. Susser explains, when they ignore the early warnings that say "enough is enough, already" and continue to work. "They discount the bodily voice that says, 'I've had enough; I want to stop.' That's when symptoms strike." If they grow accustomed to overlooking physical symptoms, serious illness or injury can result. One woman Dr. Susser treated remembered initially dismissing the pain of a stomach ache, only to be operated on later for a ruptured appendix.

Hans Selye, a noted scientist now in his 70s, is affectionately called "Dr. Stress" in honor of his pioneering research on that topic. He is still on the faculty of the University of Montreal and at his office by 7 A.M. each weekday, and only slightly later on weekends. At an age when many are content to sit in the sun, he is setting up The International Institute of Stress at that school. In a 1978 interview in *Psychology Today,* he explained his own attitude toward work and clarified the confusion surrounding what stress is and isn't:

> One striking thing we've discovered is that there are two main types of human beings: 'racehorses' who thrive on stress, and are only happy with a vigorous, fast-paced lifestyle; and 'turtles' who in order to be happy require peace, quiet and a generally tranquil environment—something that would frustrate and bore most racehorse types. I myself could hardly imagine any torture worse than having to lie on a beach doing nothing day after day. . . . We hear a great deal these days about the dangers of overwork and excessive striving, and of being the so-called Type A personality. But I think in many ways this is exaggerated and arouses unnecessary anxiety. . . . To give you a personal example, even though I am a most pronounced racehorse type, at the age of 71 I've never suffered

a heart attack or any of the usual stress-linked diseases, and I think it would be far more stressful for me to cut back my schedule—which I certainly have no intention of doing.

Workaholics are good at controlling their behavior in order to improve their physical health: One person outlined a rigid fasting regime for losing weight, and several reported that they had successfully stopped smoking. Therefore, if they decided that it would be better for them, workaholics would try to change their work habits as well. But they don't want to. Their way of working works for them. It is the familial and societal pressures to conform to the norm that create conflict, guilt, and stress—not the work itself.

Whatever physical effects workaholics experience are not from their work but rather from their feelings about it. Whatever health problems are associated with overwork are not caused by the amount of work itself. As Dr. Rhoads acknowledged in 1977 in the *Journal of the American Medical Association,* "Many persons are able to work equally long hours without becoming ill." Long hours do not cause stress. Stress appears only if those hours go against your grain.

Far from attributing any health problems to working, several of those I interviewed suspected, like Selye, that their health would suffer if they were *not* working. So workaholics have almost a physical need for the healthy stress of hard work and long hours. But what else motivates such a strong commitment to their jobs?

Although good salaries and other material rewards are often considered one of the most significant factors of a worker's attitude toward a job, they seem to make no major difference to the workaholics I interviewed. (However, although one of my respondents lived at the Y, I interviewed a relatively affluent group. Further down the socioeconomic scale, these material rewards would probably matter more.) In most cases, money matters more as a "measure of success" or a "means of keeping score" than for its buying power. As Jeno Paulucci explained, "My career goal has always been to make money ethically and honestly, not only to make money for the currency value but as a measure of success—just like someone playing golf, his scorecard is his measure of success in that game. In my game, it is making money."

At the top of the socioeconomic scale, money may become much more than a measure of mere success: It may become the measure of the person and of his accomplishments. Tax schedules alone suggest that those who wish to push their salaries over the threshold into the next bracket may be more concerned with self-worth than with net worth.

An executive secretary could not even cite a single reward she received, although, as she conceded, "I must derive something because otherwise I wouldn't be working the hours I work." Others were aware of their rewards but seemed to be largely unaffected by them. Most "complained" of having more money than they had time to spend. More than a few spent considerable sums on "buying time"—on household help and the like. One advertising executive said, "I'm not working for any rewards. I like the status and I like the money I earn but, probably, I would work just as hard anyway."

None of money's many meanings explains the workaholism of such well-paid people as Barbara Walters, Mary Wells Lawrence, and Beverly Sills. While most people will worry about earning a salary that equals their efforts, those who earn staggering salaries may feel compelled to exert themselves to justify their fat pay checks, lest anyone accuse them of being "overpaid" or "worth less," which comes uncomfortably close to "worthless." Independently wealthy workaholics may work hard for other reasons. Men may not want to be called playboys; women may not want their jobs to be thought of as playthings.

To most workaholics, psychic income—that is, responsibility, meaning, opportunity, recognition— seems more important than financial income. Several management consultants invoked the images of Superman reverting to his Clark Kent alterego or The Lone Ranger riding off into the sunset to convey the sense of triumph that accompanies the completion of an assignment. "You walk out quietly and everything's changed. That's a great feeling," was how one person put it.

This sense of power and pride also flourishes as workaholics combat a problem, accomplish the impossible in an unbelievably brief period of time, rush to the airport, and—flushed from still another victory—just make it onto the plane as the doors are

closing. Living life as a racer runs a marathon, workaholics are continually up against the clock and out
to win endurance tests of their own making. However, should they fail to meet these self-imposed
standards, they will be haunted by guilt and self-
hatred.

But if material rewards are not all that significant, then what does success really mean to a
workaholic? And does workaholism really lead to
success, as Dr. Stuart Berger, associate professor of
psychiatry at Harvard, suggests? He says that "the
workaholic is probably born obsessive—or seems to
become an obsessive soon enough—and that character structure seems to lead to success." Or does
workaholism exist and persist independently of any
accomplishments, as the experience of eminent psychologist Donald O. Hebb, 74, attests? As he wrote in
Psychology Today:

> For thirty-five years, research and the problems of
> behavior were everything to me. I loved sailing a
> small boat on the shores of Nova Scotia, where we
> went to spend a month with my parents each
> summer. But after two or three weeks, I was frankly
> anxious to get back to the lab in Montreal. I worked
> there six days a week, and did some writing on
> Sunday mornings at home. A young colleague who
> found out about this said, "I don't want to be a
> success." But he had the cart before the horse. I
> wasn't doing that to be a success. I was doing what
> I most wanted to do.

According to Richard Huber in *The American
Idea of Success*, the traditional idea of success meant

making money and translating that into status or becoming famous.

> Success was not earned by being a loyal friend or good husband. It was a reward for performance on the job. . . . It recorded a change in rank, the upgrading of a person in relation to others by the unequal distribution of money and power, prestige and fame. Yet, success was not simply *being* rich or famous. It meant *attaining* riches or *achieving* fame. You had to know where a man began and where he ended in order to determine how far he had come. How high did one have to rise to be judged a success? One measurement was to do better than your father by holding a job of higher pay or prestige. . . . Another measurement of success was having substantially a better job or making more money at the end of your working life than at the beginning.

Success, surprisingly, is not always satisfying. As actress Liv Ullman wrote in her autobiography, *Changing,* "The best thing that can come with success is the knowledge that it is nothing to long for." Dr. Berger has observed quite a few successful people at close range ("I have a number of very successful patients and a number of very successful friends"). He divides these achievers into two categories: The acute success and the chronic success.

The acute success is the person who has a "sudden windfall." A football player who wins fame in some big game is an example. His next step is to sign a contract for hundreds of thousands of dollars, and then he's approached to have his name put on underwear. The chronic success, on the other hand, proceeds consistently in a step-by-step manner that eventually leads to success.

Dr. Berger notes that those who do attain success—especially suddenly—frequently suffer a significant sense of emptiness and depression. He attributes these feelings to either guilt over having surpassed their parental levels or simply a sense of letdown. If the former is true, Huber's criterion of success (doing better than the parent) may actually be the cause of the resulting discontent. For those who "focus on a specific attainment," for instance, winning a Nobel prize, making a million dollars, or some other "consequential, concrete accomplishment," Dr. Berger suggests that feelings of failure are, to some extent, inevitable: Either they do achieve the one thing they want, leaving little else to pursue, or they don't, leaving enormous feelings of frustration and inadequacy.

Achieving a long-held goal leaves an unaccustomed void when the pursuit has been "an overwhelming, all-encompassing phenomenon." Speaking in psychoanalytic terms, Berger explains that for some, "The goal has never been worked through or understood. The pursuit *is* the source of gratification." That is, the conquest may be less satisfying than the contest. Berger contends that workaholics tend to continue to work hard after attaining significant success. "We can think of it as an expansion of the goal in order to maintain [and justify] the pursuit" and to keep up their customary tempo.

While some workaholics say they'll work less once they "make it," few do. For one thing, hard work has become a habit. For another, Staffan B. Linder, a Swedish economist, hypothesized in *The Harried Leisure Class* that success in and of itself cajoles a person into working *more* than before. Judith Bardwick, professor of psychology at the University of Michigan, surveyed successful men and found that, for them, slowing down or stopping was unlikely: "As a logical result of outstanding performance, the next steps become available."[8] That is, success increases the number of available—and attractive—offers, options, and opportunities. As Nobel laureate Dr. Rosalyn Yalow told *Newsweek,* "Before Nobel, nobody had heard of me. Now I'm much more in public view, and I can do things I've never done before."

Another possibility is that workaholics do not stop because they never *feel* successful. Their standards for success are so stringent that even astounding accomplishments are never enough. There is always a higher mountain to climb. As a result, some sense of failure is inevitable. One noted research scientist I interviewed has come close enough to have been considered a contender (and, some would allege, a campaigner) for a Nobel Prize. He has not yet won, however, and now the signs indicate that he never will. He admitted, "What I fear most is really not being right at the top of the heap. My philosophy has always been that second best is the loser." Another man, whose business has brought him fame, fortune, lucrative contracts, and high-level contacts, said, "I suppose I ought to be very happy. . . . I am getting the kind of recognition and affection that is very important to me." Still, he was not satisfied simply because he "never became a household word."

8
Workaholics:
Living with Them, Working with Them

If I were she [his wife], I would have left me long ago.
—Dan Rather

As we've seen in the last chapter, workaholics are, in general, a healthy, happy, energetic lot. But what about the people who have to keep up with their work schedules, have dinner ready for them, and try to enjoy a South Seas cruise with them? In short, what about the people who work with and live with workaholics?

Living a life of peaceful co-existence with a work addict is certainly not impossible, but that minimum return will require plenty of patience and countless compromises—all on your part. Don't expect the workaholic to reform. Workaholics may constantly make promises to change their ways, but as Dr. Susser said, "They start making what are essentially New Year's resolutions, and you know how long those last." In fact, nothing short of a major crisis even spurs them to think much about their workaholism.

Because their lives *are* their jobs, workaholics have relatively little motivation to change. So the first thing you need to decide is whether it's worth putting up with a workaholic at work or at home. If the workaholic in question happens to be your boss and the minuses outweigh the plusses, there's really not much you can do. Your best bet might be to look for another job. If, on the other hand, the workaholic in your life is someone with whom you live, then you have a harder decision. But, in this case, there's a lot you can do.

Recognizing a workaholic's addiction for what it is is an important step toward coping with it. It is *not*—no matter what the workaholic tells you— something that will change once he or she "becomes a partner," "lands that new client," or "completes this last project." Even if the workaholic in your life tries to tell you that the workaholism is temporary, tell yourself it's permanent. If the workaholic wants you to believe that he or she is only working hard in order to retire by age 35, don't listen—or at least, don't believe a word you hear.

For one thing, when those promotions come, or the accomplishments are met, or the milestones are surpassed, new ones will take their place. The top insurance agent who made the Million Dollar Round Table in the past will try for the Six Million Dollar Forum in the future; or the coveted election, promotion, or appointment will bring with it increased demands. The national sales manager has more meetings to chair, more dinners to attend, more associations to join, and more travelling to do than does the regional sales manager.

For another, what's to say that the workaholic will *want* to cut down? And even if he or she wants to, slowing down may prove impossible. What usually happens is that the workaholic's work pattern persists and the family adjusts. When (and if) a workaholic reforms, radical readjustment will be required on the family's part. As one psychologist explains, "When husbands decide to turn to their wives and kids, it's too late. They're either alienated or angry or they've adapted."

Maintaining every possible connection with the workaholic is essential. It's well worth the effort to see that you and any other family members are exposed to the workaholic's work world. Even a small child can be taken into the office, shop, or lab on a weekend. Books and toys, if available, that relate to what the workaholic does will provide some link. If the workaholic delivers mail, start a stamp collection for your child; if your spouse types, buy a toy typewriter for your tot. And so on.

Homelife can't compete with work for a workaholic but it can be made a close second. Maximize the pleasures and minimize the pressures on both of you. Don't depend on a workaholic to pick things up or drop things off; the stores may not yet be open when a workaholic goes to work and may be closed long before he gets back. But don't run yourself ragged—"let your fingers do the walking." Pay bills by telephone if this service is offered by banks in your area. Do most of your shopping from newspaper ads and catalogs and charge purchases to your account. Some stores not only deliver, but also pick up whatever you must return. These services are expected to expand as the energy shortage continues and gasoline prices soar even higher. Ordering gifts by mail or phone is even easier. You can give magazine subscriptions, theatre tickets, or museum memberships without having to buy wrapping paper, ribbon, or even a card.

Simplifying and streamlining domestic drudgery is well worth it. Try to get your workaholic spouse to lend a hand, but don't push; this is not a favorite pursuit. If you can afford it, pay someone else to do the heavy housework. And lower your standards—especially if the work is done by someone else, be it a paid employee, a professional service, your spouse (if you're lucky), or one of the kids. No floor needs to be so clean that "you could eat off it" since you never will. Don't insist that things be done your way unless your way *is* the only way. If, for example, the dishwasher will break when it's loaded incorrectly, it's worth making a fuss. Otherwise, forget it.

One couple abandoned elaborate and time-consuming meal preparation by investing in a microwave oven and buying more convenience foods. They simplified shopping, too, by buying in quantity and maintaining "inventory control" by having a set place for everything and keeping a running shopping list posted in the kitchen (for food) and the bathroom (for toiletries and cleaning products). Another woman had a standing order placed with a grocery store; every Monday, the same groceries were delivered to her door. Yes, she paid a premium for this service and, no, she couldn't take advantage of seasonal specials or succumb to a sudden whim for fresh strawberries. But, for her, the convenience was worth it.

Even young children can adjust. They need not be catered to. Why should Dad slave over the stove preparing Johnny's favorite French toast when he might be just as happy getting his own bowl of cereal, and one for Dad, too? Why should Mom chauffeur Susie to all her athletic events when she could bicycle back and forth? Where snow and ice or distance make bicycling impractical, parents might do well to lobby for schools to provide bus service or chip in to cover a charge account with a cab company rather than resort to car pools.

Sometimes your own work schedule or personal preferences preclude tagging along on the workaholic's business trip. But once in a while is fine, and even a child can be snatched out of school for an occasional trip. After all, flying over the Grand Canyon is far more educational than looking at pictures of it in a geography class. Whether the workaholic goes alone or you are travelling together, plan ahead to make the absence seem shorter. Make sure at least one picture postcard is mailed to your children before the trip starts so that it arrives while the workaholic's away instead of after he gets back. For a long trip, leave a stamped, self-addressed envelope with the children so they can send a letter or a drawing.

Take advantage of the workaholic's tendency to schedule the day by scheduling yourself into those days. Make breakfast dates and lunch dates as well as the more prosaic dinner dates. Marking these in the calendar in ink will make them almost as sacrosanct as business appointments. Plan leisure activities well in advance to avoid overcrowding an already overcommitted calendar. If possible, make monetary commitments to ensure that your plans won't be broken: Place a nonrefundable deposit on a resort weekend; invest in a ballet or symphony subscription; buy season's tickets for the hottest sports team in town; reserve a year-round tennis court. Sure, spontaneity suffers this way, but it may be the only way you'll see each other.

Insist upon vacations—you're entitled to them—but don't expect too much right away. If two weeks sounds too long, try five days the first time. If your workaholic mate has trouble going "cold turkey," limit work-related phone calls: two the first day, one the second, and none thereafter. The workaholic's co-workers will thank you. Make sure the briefcase stays home. One man purposely planned vacations that would make it impossible for his wife to work. He favored camping and cross-country skiing, which preclude bringing along any work.

Try not to squander scarce leisure time on activities that merely echo what goes on at the office. A driving, competitive worker does not need more of the same. For instance, a resort that merely offers tennis might be a better bet than a rigorous tennis camp. (Although, as we all know, the workaholic could turn even a plush resort into boot camp with a merciless, self-imposed schedule.) Also, don't waste this time socializing with people you don't really like or simply can't stand. Unpleasant associates or clients are doubtless part of the picture at work, so that kind of annoyance shouldn't be compounded at home or on vacation.

Anticipate spending a lot of time on your own. This may mean more time to "do your own thing," more time for your own work, or time to see the friends your workaholic mate can't stand. Interests and independence are critical qualities for anyone who aspires to live with a workaholic. One woman, tired of lamenting the lack of a social life and turning down other couples' invitations, just started accepting them and attending parties by herself.

Most of all, you must decide if this is really what you want. Marriage is no longer mandatory, parenthood no longer obligatory, and divorce no longer unthinkable for many, many people.

If you work for a workaholic, find out from your boss, as you would with any boss, exactly what's expected of you. Don't settle for a recitation of the standard written rules, ask co-workers about the unwritten ones as well. Find out, for example, if Brownie points are awarded for being in the office early or late. Since it's so much simpler to measure and reward attendance than performance, many bosses do just that. Learn, too, what happens when the workload builds up. Does the office gear up and hire more people, or, at least, call in temps as necessary? Establish your own authority and the budgetary limits allotted to get the work done, whether this means delegating it to someone else, calling in a consultant, or hiring a temp.

Will your hours be flexible or fairly fixed? A day that frequently runs over—even if only fifteen minutes—may play havoc with your schedule. It's one thing if you simply walk to work or drive your own car. But what if you're an exurban commuter who must catch the 6:15 P.M. train or be stranded until 10:00? What if you're a suburban commuter participating in an energy-saving car pool or van pool? If you miss the pick up, will you be stranded until the next day? Or what if you're a parent who must meet the school bus or get to the day care center at the stroke of 6 P.M.? One woman used to meet her spouse and child at the subway station, where the babystroller passed from one pair of hands to another like a flaming torch in a relay race. Tight schedules that call for split-second timing are easily disrupted.

Once on the job, set some limits. Make it clear about when—if at all—the workaholic may call you at home: only on weekdays; only until 11 A.M.; never. When requests seem unreasonable, say so. Discuss deadlines to make sure they're reasonable, too, but do so well in advance—no boss wants uncompleted work to crop up as a last-minute surprise.

Anticipate and respond to your boss' sense of urgency. True, sometimes the time pressure will be unnecessary, but sometimes there may be a real emergency. Use Express Mail for fast service. Establish an account with the most reliable messenger service in town. Memorize the telephone numbers of Federal Express and Emery Air Freight, two firms that promise overnight delivery almost anywhere. And when next-day delivery isn't soon enough, investigate the services airlines offer, if your location and your package's destination allow this alternative.

Don't forget to make sure you're suitably paid for dedication above and beyond the call of duty. Money may not matter to your workaholic boss, but it probably does to you. Negotiate for overtime, if appropriate, and for cab fares and meal money. And don't forget raises. One woman was willing to work late for a demanding boss, but she realized she could do better financially if she spent those extra hours freelancing. When she pointed this out, her next check included a fat bonus.

Financial considerations aside, you must decide if the wear and tear is worth it. Some people find fatigue a small price to pay for the excitement and experience of working for a workaholic. Others find, over time, that they're learning less and the grind is beginning to get to them. Still others decide early on that a disrupted social or family life or a complete lack of any personal life is simply too high a price to pay.

Should you decide to leave and look elsewhere, your workaholic boss may sulk because replacing you will disrupt the schedule. But don't worry. Your boss didn't get to be boss by sticking around. Your spot will be filled soon enough, even if it takes two people to do so.

If employers can accept the heretical notion that workaholism may work against them, they can cope with it in a number of ways. First, companies can make it clear that output—not hours—is what counts. In some operations, hours of work are more visible than results. Law firms, for example, use overly exact billing forms that require attorneys to account for their time to the tenth of an hour (that's six minutes). These daily diaries, along with weekend sign-in sheets, foster spending time at work simply for the sake of spending time at work. They focus on when work is done and how long it takes rather than on *what* work is accomplished and how well it is done. Professionals can and should be held accountable for achieving certain standards of productivity. Instituting formal performance appraisals and management by objectives will ensure that people work on the right things rather than busy themselves on the wrong things.

Second, by emphasizing a results orientation, organizations can teach all their employees to manage their time better. This way, fewer unnecessary hours will be spent at work. Time management, a topic that has received a lot of attention recently, is frequently the subject of seminars for executives. Those who practice its principles often achieve equal—or better—results in less time. Leading proponent Alan Lakein, author of *How to Get Control of Your Time and Your Life*, offers hundreds of maxims ("Work smarter, not harder") during his $100 one-day workshops. Quite a few organizations, including Peat, Marwick, Mitchell & Company, a "Big Eight" accounting firm, offer similar training.

Third, companies must make sure that workers do not spend too much time at work over the course of a day, year, or a lifetime. Restricting the hours of access may work. It sounds silly, but simply locking the doors may be the answer. The Japanese government launched a program encouraging workers to use their vacation time: The ministry of labor distributed leaflets extolling the virtues of vacations, but some firms had to go even further—they shut down entirely for a week or two. U.S. companies could likewise promote full utilization of vacation time. As it stands now, many workaholic employees can still accrue vast amounts of vacation time and simply convert the unused time to cash. Companies could also require that some portion of vacation time—say, two weeks—be taken at once instead of one day at a time. (Where such rules already exist—for officers of the Chase Manhattan Bank, for example—they tend to be the result of state or industry regulations rather than corporate personnel policy.)

Workaholics' unwillingness to retire (their motto might as well be "Don't stop 'til you drop") also leads to a lack of interest in leaving work. There are several feasible approaches for facilitating retirement. Companies can revise existing pension plans to reduce or remove the financial penalties incurred by electing early retirement. They could also consider part-time arrangements that would allow employees to ease into retirement, perhaps as management consultants. Corporations could also offer sabbaticals so that employees might sample retirement. There are, in addition, pre-retirement programs that aid the adjustment period. Many companies already sponsor such seminars, which usually cover both the emotional and financial aspects of planning for retirement. Leo Miller, the psychiatric social worker who manages the Polaroid Corporation's counseling department, has found that "someone who's so invested in his work that he doesn't want to retire can be helped through pre-retirement counseling."

However, one organization's retirees may comprise another company's raw recruits. Firms may want to hire reluctant retirees for part-time work and special projects. More than one firm, for instance, has hired the retired to conduct marketing research interviews among senior executives, to head up a small branch office somewhere in the Sunbelt, or to service brokerage clients who are themselves retired and now live in such communities as Palm Beach or Palm Springs.

Another approach is to recognize the problems workaholics impose and to redesign jobs accordingly. Even those executive recruiters and personnel officers who decry the detrimental effects of workaholics do little to reconcile the realistic demands of the workplace with their realizations. Some jobs are actually too large for any one individual to tackle, especially after business growth or personnel cuts have restructured departments. Reorganizing responsibilities will reduce work overload and the accompanying pressure. Sears Roebuck & Company, for instance, has instituted a four-person "office of the chairman." Other jobs simply need to be overhauled and redesigned. A well-designed job is one that simultaneously permits satisfying their personal needs, realizing their personal goals, and performing the necessary work. In far too many jobs, satisfying yourself while satisfying the organization is simply impossible.

Companies can cope with workaholism much better by recognizing that this phenomenon is more suited to some positions and functions than to others. Given their inability to work well with other people and their competitive tendencies, workaholics seem poorly suited for middle management. They are not teamplayers, they are glory-grabbers. They need and expect attention to be paid to their exploits and do not appreciate the anonymity that accompanies all but the top jobs in large organizations. They are more likely to compete than to collaborate or cooperate. They may also refuse to kowtow to corporate authority or the greater good, preferring to pursue their own interests and objectives. However, there are always exceptions, and management would do well to separate the wheat from the chaff instead of blindly believing that all workaholics are either terrific or terrible.

But, there is almost always room for workaholics in large enterprises. Since workaholics are better at creating structures than at merely carrying out orders, they are well-suited for running quasi-entrepreneurial divisions; expansions involving new technologies, new product areas, or new markets; profit centers; spun-off subsidiaries; far-flung branch operations that are far removed from headquarters' control; start-up opportunities; turnaround situations; and, of course, the chairmanship. Outside of industry, the prospects are even better. Workaholics do very well in creative endeavors, mom-and-pop enterprises, freelance fields, consulting, private practice of law and medicine, and so on.

Many firms persist in believing that workaholism is always in their best interest: few companies currently view workaholism as an actual or potential problem. After all, workaholism is often an asset because "many of those who work hard also work well." Most would still rather encourage workaholism than inhibit it, and would rather hire workaholics than fire them. As a consultant was warned before joining one of the world's most prestigious management consulting firms, "If you don't love to work, don't come here."

9
Workaholism:
Making It Work for You

*The business is an extension of me. It
should work for me. I shouldn't work for it.*
—Steven Poses

The life of leisure goes against the grain of
workaholics. They march not to the beat of a different drummer, but rather to the tick of a different
stopwatch; the alarm clock is their starter's gun.
Mental pedometers tell them how far they've come
and how far is left to go. Workaholics don't work for
or wait for the gold watch. Seldom aspiring to retire,
they work until they expire. And many would rather
die than live a life without work.

Despite the dire warnings about what workaholism can do, there are advantages. Therefore this
chapter will not tell you how to change your stripes.
For one thing, it's probably not possible. For another,
it may not be desirable. The purpose of this chapter
is to suggest methods to maximize the pleasures and
minimize the pressures of workaholism. It will offer

ways of offsetting the problems workaholism pro-
vokes so that workaholics can find fulfillment rather
than frustration. This section is about making workaholism work *for* you instead of *against* you.

What matters above all in adjusting your attitudes and activities is to acknowledge that you're a
workaholic and to accept that fact. In Dr. Selye's
terms, decide whether you're a racehorse or a turtle
and live your life accordingly. As he was quoted in
The New York Times:

> If a person is a stress seeker, and his body is falling
> apart, the last thing I would ever diagnose [sic] is
> that he be imprisoned on a beach for three
> months. . . . He will do nothing but run up and
> down the beach and think about Wall Street. . . .
> He might as well be on Wall Street.

Find the job that fits. Alan Dershowitz, a Harvard Law School professor, was quoted as saying:
"What I've been able to do and what other successful
people have been able to do is to evaluate your own
type of smarts and then make the world believe that
the right question is the one that you're best able to
answer. It's being able to shape the ballpark around
your abilities."[1]

Nothing could be more important, more obvious, or more often overlooked. Many people are
caught in careers they don't want. Are you a physician because your mother wanted you to be one, because your father wasn't one, or because you enjoy
being one? Simple self-assessment may provide the
key: What do I enjoy most? What do I enjoy least?

What parts of my job would I do for free? What is drudgery?

Sometimes all that's at fault is the most recent promotion or reorganization. Too many people have moved up the corporate ladder only to move away from what they like to do. Or they've traded working with people for working with things (or vice versa). It may not take much to get back on the right track. Sometimes activities off the job—lecturing, writing, teaching—are more appealing than those on the job. This, then, is the clue to slant your work toward what you want to do. But sometimes people are just in the wrong careers.

While it's hard to abandon an occupation for which you trained long and hard—especially if you're well-paid—many people have managed to combine what they *have* been doing with what they really want to do. Such doctor-writers as Robin Cook and Richard Selzer come to mind here. Monetary income may stay the same, sink, or soar, but psychic income always increases.

Find the place that fits. Atmosphere affects everyone, but especially workaholics, since they spend so much time at work. Someone accustomed to a plush Park Avenue address may not adapt well to a so-called "shirt sleeves" environment. One executive recruiter recalls a man who accepted a $100,000 job without seeing his future office. He transplanted his family from Connecticut to California only to quit the first day on the job. The reason? He couldn't stand the government-issue-type gray metal desks and the dirty, dingy linoleum floors. Similarly, if all your colleagues are more interested in their golf games or garden clubs than in their job you may not fit in.

Find the pace that fits. Workaholics consider the tempo of most organizations to be more or less glacial. Consider workaholism in career planning both for yourself and for your subordinates. The degree of work involvement a person wants should correspond to that demanded by the position. A workaholic in a 9-to-5 slot may be just as miserable as the 9-to-5 type who's forced to work long hours. Such preferences, if reviewed in advance, may prevent making assignments that will ultimately lead to turnover, transfer, or termination. This is best investigated in the interview. A workaholic boss is well-advised to give a realistic job preview, including a warning that "we work almost every Saturday and Sunday." Conversely, a nonworkaholic boss might mention, as one told me, "You'll make me look bad if you stay past 5 P.M."

Colleagues, in turn, are apt to find the workaholic impatient and rushed. One workaholic's secretary told me:

> If he asks me to get someone on the phone, before I can dial the first digit, he asks if I'm doing it. If I arrive early, he can't wait to give me the mail and memos he has done the night before. He asks if I'm ready to start working before I can even open my desk.

Another secretary complained that the biggest problem in working for her boss was in "dealing with the very unrealistic and unreasonable deadlines she has set."

A workaholic's haste to finish something or desire to stay late to tie up loose ends is seldom shared. Still another secretary said, "Often I am under the gun to stay late because he doesn't realize that quitting time has come and gone." Either temper your sense of time urgency or spare your staff by hiring an evening shift or temporary workers—or find employees whose willingness to work equals your own.

Create challenges in your work. As an advertising executive told me, "I wouldn't be happy in any job where I didn't feel constantly called upon to solve difficult situations and problems. If there were no problems and no frustrations, it would be dull and boring." Motivated workers respond to more work. They derive pleasure from dealing with pressure. They delight in taking on something new, tackling something unusual, doing something different. When workaholics do not feel challenged, they lose interest and become less effective.

Diversify each day. Workaholics suffer from short attention spans. Alan Lakein maintains that the people who work very hard and very long generally try to add spice to their day by doing a variety of things. Switching gears may be as refreshing for a workaholic as stopping is for someone else. Indeed, a change can be as good as a rest, and for a workaholic, probably better. Reading is a great break from meetings; writing offers a respite from reading. And both are better—and far less fattening—than coffee breaks. As noted author, producer, and television personality David Frost remarked in *US*, "I find each of my activities a relaxation from the other."

Make sure every day is different. Laurel Cutler, senior vice president of Leber Katz Partners, a New York advertising agency, says that "the joy of my job is that no two days are ever alike." Studies of sensation seeking have shown that individuals differ in the amount of variety they require. Workaholics crave continual stimulation—repetition and routine render them almost useless. They thrive on variety and quickly become bored by static situations. And as a foundation president said, "If I'm not enthusiastic, forget it."

Use your time; don't let it use you. Take advantage of your natural tendencies. Workaholics are able to get up and get going early. This pattern is probably based on a person's body temperature. According to John Palmer, a University of Massachusetts physiologist, the population really is divided into "early birds" and "night owls" whose effectiveness and efficiency follow the daily curve of their body temperature. Early birds warm up more quickly and cool off earlier than night owls.

So don't fritter your early morning energy and efficiency on unproductive tasks. This is not the right time to wade through the newspaper or open junk mail. Instead tackle those tasks that require total attention: Dictate an important memo or finish your five-year plan. You might also fit in something that is liable to get squeezed out of your schedule as the day progresses: Polish up an article you've been planning to submit to a professional journal. Exercising is another productive workday starter. Many gyms are open extra early for a before-work squash game, swim, or work-out. Starting the day actively and positively instead of wasting the time on more mundane matters also gives you an unbeatable and well-deserved sense of accomplishment that lasts all day long.

Develop systems and strategies to make the most of time. Frank Berger, whose typical day was profiled at the beginning of this book, designed his suite of offices so that he could conduct two meetings simultaneously. He bounced back and forth between them just as a doctor or dentist slips into and out of multiple examining rooms. Less expensive solutions include a car phone, speaker phone, portable phone, and other gadgets. George Lang, the restaurant consultant and critic, designed a special utensil—a combination knife and fork—so he could eat with one hand while writing with the other. Few, however, have gone as far as Peter F. Drucker, the California-based management consultant, who responds to most of his mail with an all-purpose printed reply card. It reads:

> MR. PETER F. DRUCKER
>
> GREATLY APPRECIATES YOUR KIND INTEREST, BUT IS UNABLE TO:
> CONTRIBUTE ARTICLES OR FOREWORDS; COMMENT ON MANUSCRIPTS OR
> BOOKS; TAKE PART IN PANELS AND SYMPOSIA; JOIN COMMITTEES OR
> BOARDS OF ANY KIND; ANSWER QUESTIONNAIRES; GIVE
> INTERVIEWS; AND APPEAR ON RADIO OR TELEVISION.

But don't get carried away. Mounting a TV set on a stationary exercise bicycle, rigging a reading light on an electric jogger, reading or writing while driving, or carrying a special key to convert your office elevator to a nonstop express are a bit too much.

Eliminate inefficiencies. Figure out what you do that's a waste of time. Do you answer letters that don't require a response, or are some of the replies so similar that a form letter would do? Do you do things at the wrong time? Placing calls between noon and 2:00 is generally fruitless; you may be at your desk but the person you're calling is probably at lunch. Do you tend to do things too early? Washing the floor at 3 P.M. when the kids will track in dirt an hour later sets yourself up for frustration as well as repeat performances.

Don't deliberate excessively on decisions that don't warrant the attention. Become decisive or decide not to decide. Time *is* money, but it's also much scarcer than money for some. Child psychologist Dr. Lee Salk no longer deliberates when he shops for shoes and shirts. Taking the time to decide which of two items to buy, he calculates, will cost him more than buying both. And once you've made a decision, forget about it. It's done.

Let others do things for you. Just as with delegating, workaholics have a hard time letting go. They equate it, incorrectly, with giving up or losing control. If you're the one who always takes the initiative in setting up meetings and conferences, give someone else a chance. If you habitually interview and entertain prospective employees, let a subordinate sit in on the interviews and take them to lunch, too.

Even workaholics can come to regard some aspects of their work with dread instead of their customary delight. Are you the chairman of a committee you no longer care about? Resign and recommend someone else in your stead. Part of the reason why workaholics may find themselves with unwanted work is because they have difficulty saying "No." Since it is far better to decline at the outset than to back out later on, learn to avoid any commitment you won't want to keep. One wag suggests inventing an all-purpose excuse along the lines of "I'd like to, but I'm expecting a visit from my mother-in-law then." Or practice referring requests. Prepare a list of names and actually rehearse, if necessary, so you'll be ready. If you're a full professor who gets frequent offers to review books or manuscripts, suggest a junior colleague or even a graduate student who could use the experience, the exposure, and the money.

Delegate, delegate, delegate. Don't make the same mistakes as Arthur Kurlansky, president of a New Hampshire ad agency. "I insisted that everything go through me, at every stage," explains Kurlansky. "I made every decision, the big ones and the little ones—who plowed the driveway, whether the type in the ad should be blue or green, who to hire, and who to fire." Now Kurlansky has decided to let the other people in his agency do a lot more. He has successfully delegated some of the selecting and much of the screening of new employees. "Art directors are really better judges of art directors than I am," Kurlansky concedes. "I let the secretaries do their own interviewing. They look at the résumés. Then they give me three candidates and their opinions."[2]

Work alone or hire only other workaholics. Workaholics are often intolerant of people they work with and impatient as well. The difficulty encountered in coordinating schedules with another person has led more than one workaholic to work alone. Dr. Salk wrote his first book with a co-author, but went on to write several others by himself. He found that "it took more time to work with a co-author than to do it alone." Dr. Elizabeth Whelan thinks that choosing to work on her own "was the best decision I ever made. I can work without being inhibited by anyone else's schedule."

Both Salk and Whelan also work at home. This eliminates commuting time but works only if you have the self-discipline (or the staff) to work despite a sink full of dirty dishes. It also means having to purchase what most people miss most about offices, such as Xerox machines and WATS lines.

Become a mentor. In *The Seasons of a Man's Life,* Daniel J. Levinson uses the term "mentor" to mean teacher, sponsor, adviser, and more: a host and a guide, an exemplar, a counselor. A good mentor, explains Dr. Levinson, combines the best qualities of both a good parent and a good friend. He represents all that the other person hopes to acquire and achieve: skill, knowledge, accomplishment.

"Adopt" a younger person at your *alma mater,* in your company, in your professional organization, or elsewhere. Share what you've learned on the way up and what you wish you'd known when you were at the bottom. And put this person in touch with your contact network, since your protégé probably would love to know these people, yet might never get to meet them otherwise.

As good teachers have long known, it is not always clear who gains more, the student or the professor. So it is with mentoring. You have a chance to learn what the next generation is thinking and to contribute to what that generation becomes. It is not easy, but its satisfactions are strong. Mentoring need not take a lot of time, but it can be worth more than whatever time it takes.

Make sure you make time for what matters to you. Decide if you want your family to feel that they're last on your list. You really *are* more indispensable to those at home than you are to those at work. Try to put things in perspective. Your parents will appreciate your presence at their golden anniversary party more than your colleagues will miss you at a company dinner. Your son or daughter's wedding is a once-in-a-lifetime occasion; your company's annual meeting will, by definition, be repeated next year.

When it comes to family life, it's not just the big events but the everyday activities that count. Just as an out-of-the-blue present seems more special than one that comes on an anniversary or birthday, showing up to watch your child's basketball team practice counts more than merely making the championship game. Try to pitch in and take responsibility, too, for daily drudgery—not just for the Thanksgiving dinner or the Fourth of July picnic. And don't expect medals for doing what you should. While complaints are all too audible, appreciation is often sadly silent; nonetheless, it is there.

You're entitled to enjoy yourself, too. Leisure is legitimate. Resume a favorite hobby from your youth. Try folk dancing or fencing, for instance, and then see if you want to continue with it. Read books that are totally unrelated to your work. Try science fiction, for instance, or pick up Shakespeare. Turn on a TV show. Make new friends or renew contact with forgotten friends. Flip through your Rolodex and arrange a strictly social lunch with a business associate you actually like.

Be sure to set aside some time, too, to be spent in solitude and silence. Meditate, pray, or take a walk in the woods. Block off your calendar. Reserve a whole day, a half-day, or even an hour for yourself at regular intervals. Instruct your secretary not to schedule any appointments during the times you set aside and tell the switchboard to hold all calls.

Get professional help if you need it. If your addiction starts to seem more like an affliction, evaluate the role of work in your life. Dr. Prout claims that "workaholics can change," although he concedes that such a transformation is accomplished only "with difficulty." Typically, a workaholic will not seek help until confronted by some crisis:

• a crisis on the job, where the boss might have said, "Stop screaming at the secretaries," or where the workaholic is passed over for a promotion.

• a crisis at home, where his spouse might have said, "Stop answering the phone when we're making love," or where there is an obvious problem with the children.

• a crisis of health, where the physician has said, "Your electrocardiogram doesn't look good," or where the workaholic has already had a full-fledged heart attack.

In the course of therapy, Dr. Prout encourages workaholics to explore the activities they enjoyed as adolescents and to try to return to or recapture them. With couples, he seeks to open lines of communication, to explore the games people are playing, and to examine the rules—both covert and overt—that are operating. "I ask them what life was like when they were engaged. Generally, it was different. For all of us it is. But for these people, it's a dramatic change."

Should such a change in life-style prove desirable—and it may well be necessary to stave off death or divorce—there is some evidence, albeit more anecdotal than academic, to suggest it can be done. In 1977, Dr. John Rhoads cited the efficiency of certain radical remedies and readjustments in *The Journal of the American Medical Association:* "Correction involved enforced rest, therapy that may vary from counseling to hospitalization, and specialized treatment."

One workaholic who undertook such a change is Lisa Richette, a 50-ish Philadelphia judge who, before her treatment, also taught at Temple University Law School and lectured widely. Earlier, she wouldn't allow herself to go at "less than full speed": "I never took a lunch hour. I gulped a sandwich while I read and dictated letters. I thought it was so clever—making use of every moment."[3]

However, after a period of severe depression in 1978, she underwent several weeks of intensive therapy. Upon her return, she cut down on commitments, curtailed her hours, and curbed her coffee consumption as well. Richette revels in the results. She no longer equates her worth with her work. The "I am what I do" attitude is gone.

In Darrell Sifford's case, it was divorce that led him to convert. Sifford is a syndicated columnist whose articles appear in *The Philadelphia Inquirer* and over sixty other daily papers. Sifford, now in his late 40s, says that his marriage was broken in large measure by too many twenty-hour days and too many seven-day weeks. The divorce convinced him to try to put his work in perspective. The change has lowered his blood pressure, caused his friends and colleagues to "like me a helluva lot better," and given him "a better outlook" on life. But the biggest change and the surest sign that he has "recovered" is that this career newspaperman now not only goes away without taking any work with him, but finds that when on vacation "I don't even read a newspaper."

Another man found that radical reasons or remedies weren't required. All it apparently took one New York banker to change his ways was the realization "that there's more to life than work" and of what his work might bring:

> Nobody (especially in these large institutions) will care or appreciate your efforts after you "kill" yourself for them. At best, you'll get a notation in the house organ and some sympathy cards sent to your family.

His case brings to mind the question of "burn-out," of suddenly slowing down or dropping out. Dr. Harold M. Visotsky, chairman of the psychiatry department at Northwestern University, told *Chicago Tribune* reporter Ronald Kotulak, "There has been a very significant increase in the pressure that people in all levels of management have to face, and it is leading to executive burnouts." Of the workaholics I interviewed, many of their careers—management consulting, journalism, investment banking—are referred to colloquially (if sexistly) as "young men's games." Yet I saw many who were still going strong well past the point at which they could conceivably be called young. Here again, it would be helpful to have talked with the same set of people at several points in their lives.

Another workaholic resorted to simple strategems to "cure" his workaholism, but apparently with less success. Wayne E. Oates, a theologian on the faculty of the University of Louisville (Kentucky) School of Medicine, described a series of ways to combat workaholism in *Workaholics, Make Laziness Work for You*. However, despite Oates' documented attempts to reform, he appears to have reverted. In an earlier book about workaholics, *Confessions of a Workaholic*, he claimed he was a converted workaholic. But in his second book, named above, he calls himself a confirmed workaholic.

For most workaholics, workaholism appears to be a permanent personality trait. Without longitudinal data, it is impossible to pinpoint its onset or predict its duration. Yet the characteristic willingness to work is present in childhood and adolescence, long before workaholics even enter the labor force. Their work behavior remains consistent, despite even drastic career changes. And lastly, their reluctance to retire adds credence to the theory of permanence.

While the majority of workers narrowly define their jobs with such statements as "That's not my department," workaholics, in contrast, show initiative and strive to individualize and enlarge their areas of purview. With an uncanny ability to see new opportunities in even the most commonplace situations, workaholics happily—if compulsively—seize upon them to subtly mold the job to better suit themselves.

Then the distinction between what is work and what is not work begins to blur. To the observer, everything workaholics do appears to be work; to workaholics, all that they do is enjoyable. This problem of perspective is a persistent one when it comes to defining work or deciding what "counts." Walter Neff, professor emeritus of psychology at New York University, observes: "Mountaineering may be a very arduous activity, but it is play for the tourist and work for the guide."[4]

Having abandoned the traditional boundaries between what is work and what is play, workaholics can function in a single, integrated, and coherent way. They need not be one person at work and another at home or away. They avoid the steady interpersonal and intrapsychic strain that can result from a compartmentalized life. They don't need to behave or talk differently as they move between settings or roles. When work is a joy and not just a job, it is never odious or arduous. Having achieved an intimacy or identity with work, workaholics are neither able to nor interested in separating or segregating work from the rest of their life. Observers may be distressed by the "sad plight" of workaholics, by their chronic "affliction." But, most workaholics won't understand what all the commotion is about. Instead, they would agree with Winston Churchill, who once said, "Those whose work and pleasures are one are fortune's favorite children."

Notes

CHAPTER 1

1. Robert L. Kahn, "On the meaning of work," *Journal of Occupational Medicine* 16 (1974):716.
2. Lotte Bailyn, "Involvement and accommodation in technical careers: An inquiry into the relation to work at mid-career." In *Organizational Careers: Some New Perspectives,* ed. John Van Maanen (London: Wiley, 1977).
3. John M. Rhoads, "Overwork," *Journal of the American Medical Association* 237 (1977):2615.
4. Roger Rapoport, *The Super-Doctors* (Chicago: Playboy Press, 1975), p. 118.
5. Lindsy Van Gelder, "Ellen Goodman: The columnist you can trust," *Ms.,* March 1979, p. 54.
6. Doris Kearns, *Lyndon Johnson and the American Dream* (New York: Signet, 1976), p. 2.

CHAPTER 2

1. Edith Loew Gross, "The all-out, attractive style of Mary Wells Lawrence;" *Vogue,* February 1978, p. 200.
2. Kathleen Madden, "Barbara Walters," *Vogue,* June 1975, p. 145.

CHAPTER 3

1. Meyer Friedman and Ray M. Rosenman, *Type A Behavior and Your Heart* (Greenwich, CT: Fawcett Crest, 1974).
2. David C. Glass, "Stress, competition and heart attacks," *Psychology Today,* December 1976, p. 57.

CHAPTER 4

1. Robert D. Caplan and Kenneth W. Jones, "Effects of work load, role ambiguity and Type A personality on anxiety, depression and heart rate," *Journal of Applied Psychology* 60 (6) (1975):713.
2. Lawrence Rout, "A risk arbitrageur plays dangerous game of betting on mergers," *The Wall Street Journal*, February 22, 1979, p. 21.

CHAPTER 5

1. Douglas T. Hall and Samuel Rabinowitz, "Caught up in work," *The Wharton Magazine* 2(1) (1977):19–25.

CHAPTER 6

1. Ronald Kotulak, "Anybody here seen a work addict?" *Chicago Tribune Magazine*, December 31, 1972, p. 14.
2. Virginia E. Johnson and William H. Masters, "Contemporary influences on sexual response: The work ethic," *The Journal of School Health* 46(4) (1976):211, 212.
3. Fred Kirsch, "The non-stop Fields have done a PR job on life," *Sunday Record*, February 6, 1977, p. 12.
4. Warren Boroson, "The workaholic in you," *Money*, June 1976, p. 32.

CHAPTER 7

1. Wardell B. Pomeroy, *Dr. Kinsey and the Institute for Sex Research* (New York: Harper & Row, 1972), pp. 435–438.
2. Enid Nemy, "Fashions charted on a yacht's deck," *The New York Times*, August 4, 1977, p. C1.
3. Willis J. Goudy, Edward A. Powers, and Patricia Keith,

"Work and retirement: A test of attitudinal relationships," *Journal of Gerontology* 30(2) (1975):193–198.

4. Rose DeWolf, "Hell no, we won't go," *Discover* (The Philadelphia *Bulletin* magazine), February 8, 1976, p. 6.

5. J. Roger O'Meara, "Retirement," *Across the Board*, January 1977, pp. 4, 9.

6. Ronald Kotulak, "The executive game: Stress illness tarnishes prize," *Chicago Tribune*, March 25, 1979, Sec. 1, p. 8.

7. Clinton G. Weiman, "A study of occupational stressors and the incidence of disease/risk," *Journal of Occupational Medicine* 19(2) (1977):119–122.

8. Judith Bardwick, "The dynamics of successful people," *New Research on Women*, 1974, p. 88.

CHAPTER 9

1. Mary Alice Kellogg, *Fast Track* (New York: McGraw-Hill, 1978), p. 52.

2. Susan Benner, "Stress: How one CEO is learning to cope with it," *INC.*, October 1979, pp. 58, 60.

3. Darrell Sifford, " 'Superwoman' learns to watch her flowers grow," *The Philadelphia Inquirer*, September 24, 1978, p. 1K.

4. Walter S. Neff, "Psychoanalytic conceptions of the meaning of work," *Psychiatry* 28(4) (1965):328.

Bibliography

Abeel, E. Hers. *The New York Times*, February 8, 1979, p. C2.

Abrahms, J.L. "Irrational, maladaptive cognitions and behaviors of the super insurance producer." *CLU Journal*, July 1979, p. 34.

Anderson, L. "The ABC's of Leonard Gordenson." *W*, September 16–23, 1977, p. 21.

Appleton, J., and W. Appleton. *How Not To Split Up.* New York: Berkley, 1979.

Archer, J. *The Executive "Success."* New York: Grosset & Dunlap, 1969.

Aring, C.D. "Work." *American Journal of Psychiatry* 131–8(1974):901–902.

Baer, J. "Do you have too much to do?" *Woman's Day*, May 1976, p. 74.

Bailyn, L., and E.H. Schein. "Life/career considerations as indicators of quality of employment." In *Measuring Work Quality for Social Reporting*, ed. by A.D. Biderman and T.F. Drury. New York: Sage, 1976.

Baker, R. "Those well-ground noses." *The New York Times*, March 25, 1973, p. 15.

Balchin, N. "Satisfactions in work." *Occupational Psychology* 44 (1970):165–173.

Bartolemé, F. "Executives as human beings." *Harvard Business Review*, November–December 1972, p. 62.

Bell, A. "Asexual chic: Everybody's not doing it." *Village Voice*, January 23, 1978, p. 1.

Bell, D. "The clock watchers: Americans at work." *Time*, September 8, 1975, pp. 55–57.

———. *Work and Its Discontents.* Boston: Beacon Press, 1958.

Bellah, R.N. "To kill and survive or to die and become: The active life and the contemplative life as ways of being adult." *Daedalus,* Spring 1976, p. 57.

Bem, D.J. *Beliefs, Attitudes and Human Affairs.* Belmont, CA: Brooks/Cole, 1970.

Benchley, N. *The Benchley Roundup.* New York: Harper & Row, 1954.

Bender, M. *At the Top.* New York: Doubleday, 1975.

Benner, S. "Stress." *INC.,* October 1979, p. 56.

Bennetts, L. "Doctors' wives: Many report marriage is a disappointment." *The New York Times,* May 7, 1979, p. B10.

———. "Fabrics: His life and art." *The New York Times,* March 30, 1978, p. C1.

———. "The Vermeils: She accepts the waiting." *The* [Philadelphia] *Sunday Bulletin,* November 27, 1977, Sec. 4, p. 1.

Berger, P. "Making it happen at the Garden." *The New York Times Magazine,* September 30, 1978, p. 17.

Berger, P.L. (Ed.). *The Human Shape of Work.* New York: Macmillan, 1964.

Bernard, J. *The Future of Marriage.* New York: World, 1972.

Bird, C. The Two-Paycheck Marriage. New York: Rawson, Wade. 1979.

Birmingham, F.A. "Work-a-holics live longer." *The Saturday Evening Post,* March 1979, p. 38.

"Blackout II—an eerie slowdown." *The New York Times,* July 17, 1977, Sec. 3, p. 15.

Bortner, R.W. "A short rating scale as a potential measure of pattern A behavior." *Journal of Chronic Diseases* 22(1969):87–91.

Botwin, C. "Is there sex after marriage?" *The New York Times Magazine,* September 16, 1979.

Bralove, M. "For married couples, two careers can be an exercise in frustration." *The Wall Street Journal,* May 13, 1975, p. 1.

Bray, D.W., R.J. Campbell, and D.L. Grant. *Formative*

Years in Business. New York: Wiley, 1974.

Brody, J. "Studies asking: 'Who's happy?' " *The New York Times,* January 16, 1979, p. C2.

Brooks, J. (Ed.) *The Autobiography of American Business.* Garden City: Anchor, 1975.

Brown, H.G. "Step into my parlor." *Cosmopolitan,* August 1977, p. 6.

Brown, L. "Salant move raises issue of loyalty." *The New York Times,* March 29, 1979, p. C21.

Brozan, N. "Stress at work: The effects on health." *The New York Times,* June 14, 1979, p. C1.

Broy, A. "The Work-Obsessed." *The New York Times,* December 19, 1971.

Bryant, C.D. (Ed.) *The Social Dimensions of Work.* Englewood Cliffs: Prentice-Hall, 1972.

Bulkeley, W.B. "Chrysler's Riccardo uses tough approach to attack firm's ills." *The Wall Street Journal,* July 7, 1976, p. 1.

Buskirk, R.H. *Your Career.* New York: New American Library, 1977.

Butensky, A., V. Faralli, D. Heebner, and I. Waldron. "Elements of coronary-prone behavior pattern in children and teenagers." *Journal of Psychosomatic Research* 20(1976):439–444.

Buzzard, R.B. "A practical look at industrial stress." *Occupational Psychology* 47(1973):51–61.

Cantarow, E. "Women workaholics." *Mother Jones,* June 1979, p. 56.

Caplowe, T. *The Sociology of Work.* New York: McGraw-Hill, 1954.

Carlisle, D. "Music biz: She's a hit." *Working Woman,* October 1978, p. 22.

Caro, R. *The Power Broker.* New York: Knopf, 1974.

Cherns, A.B. "Better working lives: A social scientist's view." *Occupational Psychology* 47(1973):23–28.

Cherry, L. "On the real benefits of stress." *Psychology Today,* March 1978, p. 60.

Cohen, L. "In defense of the workaholic." *Cosmopolitan,* July 1978, p. 140.

Coles, R. *Privileged Ones.* Boston: Atlantic–Little, Brown, 1977.

Colligan, D. "That helpless feeling: The dangers of stress." *New York,* July 14, 1975, pp. 28–30.

Croyden, M. "When the telephone rang, did you know it meant war?" *The New York Times,* August 14, 1977, Sec. 2, p. 1.

Csikszentmihalyi, M. *Beyond Boredom and Anxiety.* San Francisco: Jossey-Bass, 1975.

Cunniff, J. "Expert on 'workaholics' says country needs more." *The Bulletin,* August 1979, p. 18.

———. "In defense of workaholics." *The New York Post,* April 23, 1979, p. 39.

Curtis, C. "They can't be 'workaholics'—they're having too much fun." *The New York Times,* March 30, 1975, Sec. 1, p. 38.

Darrach, B. "It's an Asimovalanche! The one-man book-a-month club has just published his 179th." *People,* November 22, 1976, p. 110.

DeGrazia, S. *Of Time, Work, and Leisure.* New York: Twentieth Century Fund, 1962.

Deutsch, C. "The workaholic spouse." *Parents,* March 1979, p. 36.

Dexter, L.A. *Elite and Specialized Interviewing.* Evanston, IL: Northwestern University Press, 1970.

Dickson, P. *The Future of the Workplace.* New York: Weybright & Talley, 1975.

Donnelly, C. "How hard should you work?" *Money,* April 1975, p. 89.

Dorfman, D. "Overnight highflier." *Esquire,* August 15, 1978, p. 9.

"Do you work too hard?" *U.S. News & World Report,* March 26, 1979, p. 73.

Drabble, M. "Busy busy busy busy busy." *The New York Times*, August 6, 1977, p. 17.

Dranov, P. "Washington's workaholics." *Family Weekly*, September 25, 1977, p. 8.

Drill, H. "At the top, it's up early, stay late." *The Bulletin*, February 12, 1978.

Drucker, P.F. *The Effective Executive*. New York: Harper & Row, 1958.

———. *Management*. New York: Harper & Row, 1973.

———. "How to manage your time." *Harper's*, December 1976, p. 57.

Dubin, R. "Industrial workers' worlds." *Social Problems* 3(1956):131–142.

———. *The World of Work*. Englewood Cliffs: Prentice-Hall, 1958.

Durant, H.W. *The Problem of Leisure*. London: Routledge, 1938.

Eckman, F.M. "The Joy of Overwork," *The New York Post*, February 26, 1977, p. 21.

Ekerdt, D.J., C.L. Ross, R. Bosse, and P.T. Costa. "Longitudinal change in preferred age of retirement." *Journal of Occupational Psychology* 49 (1976):161–169.

Elizur, D., and A. Tziner. "Vocational needs, job rewards and satisfaction: A canonical analysis." *Journal of Vocational Behavior* 10 (1977):205–211.

Elliott, O. *Men at the Top*. New York: Harper & Bros., 1959.

Engel, P.H. *The Overachievers*. New York: The Dial Press, 1976.

Engstrom, T.W., and D.J. Juroe. *The Work Trap*. Old Tappan, N.J.: Revell, 1979.

Ephron, D. "Laziness in the world's busiest city." *New York*, August 14, 1978. p. 26.

"Executive stress may not be all bad." *Business Week*, April 30, 1979, p. 96.

Farney, D. "For high-level aides in Washington, it is all work, no family." *The Wall Street Journal,* January 30, 1979, p. 1.

Feinberg, M.R. "The corporate bigamist." *Across the Board,* November 1976, p. 61.

————. "The truth about executive stress." *Dun's Review,* August 1964, p. 34.

Feinberg, M.R., and R.F. Dempewolff, *Corporate Bigamy.* New York: Morrow, 1980.

Feinberg, S. "Workaholics: In a class apart from hard workers." *Women's Wear Daily,* October 5, 1977, pp. 42–43.

Fillenbaum, G.G., and G.L. Maddox. "Work after retirement." *The Gerontologist* 14(5) (1974):418–424.

Firestone, R. *The Success Trip.* Chicago: Playboy Press, 1976.

Fiske, D.W., and S. Maddi. *Functions of Varied Experience.* Homewood, IL: The Dorsey Press, 1961.

Florman, S.E. "The job-enrichment mistake." *Harper's,* May 1976, p. 18.

Fortino, D. "Sex-drive slowdown." *Harper's Bazaar,* August 1979, p. 52.

French, J.R.P., Jr., and R.D. Caplan. "Organizational stress and individual strain." In *The Failure of Success,* ed. by A.J. Marrow. New York: AMACOM, 1972.

Fried, M.A. "Is work a career?" *Trans-Action,* September–October, p. 66.

Friedan, B. *The Feminine Mystique.* New York: Norton, 1963.

Friedman, A., and R.J. Havighurst. "Work and retirement." In *Man, Work and Society,* ed. by S. Nosow and W.H. Form. New York: Basic Books, 1962.

Friedmann, G. *The Anatomy of Work.* London: Heinemann, 1961.

Fromme, A. "The workaholic." *Cosmopolitan,* November 1973, p. 194.

Gaylin, W. *Feelings.* New York: Harper & Row, 1979.

Gechman, A.S. "Without work, life goes. . . ." *Journal of Occupational Medicine* 16(11) (1974):749–751.

Ginzberg, E., and J.L. Herma. *Talent and Performance.* New York: Columbia University Press, 1964.

Glasser, W. *Positive Addiction.* New York: Harper & Row, 1976.

Goertzel, M.G., V. Goertzel, and T.G. Goertzel. *Three Hundred Eminent Personalities.* San Francisco: Jossey-Bass, 1978.

Goldberg, L. "Overtime: The long, hard day of successful New Yorkers." *New York,* November 25, 1974, p. 47.

Goode, W.J. "A theory of role strain." *American Sociological Review* 25 (1960):483–496.

Gorey, H. *Nader.* New York: Grosset & Dunlap, 1975.

Gowler, D., and K. Legge. *Managerial Stress.* New York: Wiley, 1975.

Greenberg, P.S. "Work addicts." *American Way,* December 1977, p. 39.

Greene, G. "Cafe des artistes: If it's good enough for George." *New York,* January 19, 1976, p. 70.

Gross, A. "Psyching yourself up." *Mademoiselle,* April 1976, p. 158.

Gross, E.L. "Nancy Kissinger—Out front in the best American style." *Vogue,* June 1979, p. 188.

"Growing dissatisfaction with 'workaholism.' " *Business Week,* February 27, 1978, p. 97.

Gunther, M. *The Very, Very Rich and How They Got That Way.* Chicago: Playboy Press, 1972.

Guzzardi, W., Jr. *The Young Executives.* New York: New American Library, 1965.

Hackman, J.R. "Work design." In *Improving Life at Work,* ed. by J.R. Hackman and J.L. Suttle. Santa Monica, CA: Goodyear, 1977.

Hackman, J.R., and G.R. Oldham. "The job diagnostic survey: An instrument for the diagnosis of jobs and the evaluation of job redesign projects." Technical Report No. 4, Department of Administrative Sciences, Yale University, May 1974.

Hailey, S. *I Married a Bestseller*. New York: Bantam, 1978.

Halberstam, D. *The Powers That Be*. New York: Knopf, 1979.

Hall, D.T. *Careers in Organizations*. Pacific Palisades, CA: Goodyear, 1976.

Hall, F.S., and D.T. Hall. *The Two-Career Couple*. Reading, MA: Addison-Wesley, 1979.

Hanson, K. "Are you working too hard? Test yourself." *The New York Daily News*, August 28, 1977, p. 5.

"Happy work," *Glamour*, January 1976, p. 24.

Hargens, L.L. "Relations between work habits, research technologies, and eminence in science." *Sociology of Work and Occupations* 5–1(1978):97–112.

Harmon, C.W. "Louis L'Amour: Fastest novel in the West." *Los Angeles*, March 1979, p. 244.

Harrington, A. *Life in the Crystal Palace*. New York: Knopf, 1959.

Harry, J. "Work and leisure." In *Sociology of Leisure*, ed. by B. Johannis, Jr., and C.N. Bull. Beverly Hills: Sage Publications, 1971.

Hatterer, L.J. "Work identity: A psychotherapeutic dimension." *American Journal of Psychiatry* 122–11(1966):1284–1286.

Hebb, D.O. "On watching myself get old." *Psychology Today*, November 1978.

Heckscher, A., and S. DeGrazia. "Executive leisure." *Harvard Business Review*, July–August 1959, p. 6.

Heller, J. *Something Happened*. New York: Knopf, 1974.

Heller, R. *The Great Executive Dream*, New York: Delacorte, 1972.

Hendrick, I. "The discussion of the instinct to master." *Psychoanalytic Quarterly* 12(1943):516–565.

Heneman, H.G., Jr. "Work and nonwork: Historical perspectives. In *Work and Nonwork in the Year 2001*, ed. by M.D. Dunette. Monterey, CA: Brooks/Cole, 1973.

Henle, P. "Leisure and the long work week." *Monthly Labor Review*, July 1966, p. 721.

Herman, R. "Guy Lafleur is all work." *The New York Times*, May 15, 1978, p. c1.

Higdon, H. *The Business Healers*. New York: Random House, 1969.

Hodenfield, C. " Two-star final." *Rolling Stone*, April 8, 1976, p. 52.

Holmstrom, L.L. *The Two-Career Family*. Cambridge: Schenkman, 1972.

Horn, J. "Bored to sickness." *Psychology Today*, November 1975, p. 92.

Horn, P. "Stress and longevity: The thriving top executive." *Psychology Today* 8(3)(1974):30.

House, J. "Occupational stress and physical health." *Manpower*, October 1973, p. 3.

"How to make the most of your time." *U.S. News & World Report*, December 3, 1973, p. 45.

Huber, R.M. *The American Idea of Success*. New York: McGraw-Hill, 1971.

"If you suffer from chronic fatigue." *U.S. News & World Report*, May 14, 1979, p. 27.

"If you think you're working too hard." *U.S. News & World Report*, July 29, 1974, p. 31.

Janis, I. *Psychological Stress*. New York: Academic Press, 1974.

Johnson, H.J. *Executive Life Styles*. New York: Life Extension Foundation, 1974.

Kahn, E.J., Jr. "Resources and responsibilities—I & II." *The New Yorker*, January 9, 1965, p. 37; January 16, 1965, p. 40.

Kahn, R.L., D.M. Wolfe, R.P. Quinn, and J.D. Snoek. *Organizational Stress*. New York: Wiley, 1964.

Kalb, M., and B. Kalb. *Kissinger*. Boston: Little, Brown, 1974.

Kando, T.M., and W.C. Summers. "The impact of work on leisure." In *Sociology of Leisure*, ed. by T.B. Johannis, Jr., and C.N. Bull. Beverly Hills: Sage Publications, 1971.

Kanter, R.M. *Men and Women of the Corporation*. New York: Basic Books, 1977.

————. *Work and Family in the United States: A Critical Review and Agenda for Research and Policy*. New York: Russell Sage Foundation, 1977.

————. "Work in a new America." *Daedalus*, Winter 1978, pp. 47–78.

Keerdoja, E. "A Nobel woman's hectic pace." *Newsweek*, October 29, 1979, 21E.

Kerr, W. *The Decline of Pleasure*. New York: Simon & Schuster, 1962.

Kiev, A. *A Strategy for Handling Executive Stress*. Chicago: Nelson-Hall, 1974.

King, D. and K. Levine. *The Best Way in the World for a Woman to Make Money*. New York: Rawson, Wade, 1979.

Kish, G.B., and W. Busse. "Correlates of stimulus-seeking." *Journal of Consulting and Clinical Psychology* 32(6)(1968):633–637.

Kohn, M.L., and C. Scholler. "Occupational experience and psychological functioning: An assessment of reciprocal effects." *American Sociological Review* 38(1)(1973):97–118.

Korda, M. *Power*. New York: Random House, 1975.

Kramer, R. "Screen queens." *Working Woman*, August 1979, p. 37.

Kramer, Y. "Work compulsion—A psychoanalytic study." *The Psychoanalytic Quarterly* 46(3)(1977):361–385.

Kurtz, P, "Should you live to work or work to live?" *New Woman*, July-August 1979, p. 48.

Lakein, A. *How To Get Control of Your Time and Your Life.* New York: New American Library, 1973.
———. *It's About Time.* New York: Bantam, 1975.

Lamson, N.W. "Block trader at Salomon." *The New York Times*, November 9, 1975, III, p. 9.

Landay, J.M. "Eating our lives up with work." *The New York Times*, November 9, 1974, p. 31.

Lawler, E.E., III. "Reward systems." In *Improving Life at Work*, ed. by J.R. Hackman and J.L. Suttle. Santa Monica, CA: Goodyear, 1977.

Lawler, E.E., III, and D.T. Hall. "The relationship of job characteristics to job involvement, satisfaction and intrinsic motivation. *Journal of Applied Psychology* 54(1970):305–312.

Lear, F. "Work is not a four-letter word." *Newsweek*, October 24, 1977, p. 22.

Leff, L. "Leisure consultants are part Dr. Freud and part Dear Abby." *The Wall Street Journal.* September 12, 1978, p. 1.

Levinson, D.J. *The Seasons of a Man's Life.* New York: Knopf, 1978.

Levinson, H. *Executive Stress.* New York: Harper & Row, 1970.
———. *Psychological Man.* Cambridge: The Levinson Institute, 1976.
———. "The abrasive personality at the office." *Psychology Today*, May 1978, p. 78.

Linder, S. *The Harried Leisure Class.* New York: Columbia University Press, 1970.

Locke, E.A. "What is job satisfaction?" *Organizational Behavior and Human Performance* 4(1969):309–336.

Lodahl, T.M., & M. Kejner. "The definition and measurement of job involvement." *Journal of Applied Psychology* 49(1)(1965):24–33.

Lyons, H. "Fascinating manhood." *Ms.* October 1975, p.62.

MacArthur, J. "The early bird not only gets the worm but also a better job." *The Wall Street Journal,* September 20, 1977, p. 1.

Maccoby, M. *The Gamesman.* New York: Simon & Schuster, 1976.

Machlowitz, M.M. Book review. *Across the Board,* January 1979, p. 31.

——. "Determining the effects of workaholism." Unpublished doctoral dissertation. Yale University, 1978.

——. "The workaholic." Unpublished master's thesis. Yale University, 1976.

——. "Workaholics." *Across the Board,* October 1977, p. 30.

——. "Workaholics: Fortune's favorite children." *New Woman,* November-December 1979, p. 59.

——. "Workaholism: What's wrong with being married to your work?" *Working Woman,* May 1978, p. 50.

——. "Working the 100-hour week—and loving it." *The New York Times,* October 3, 1976, Sec. 3, p. 3.

Mackenzie, R.A. *The Time Trap.* New York: McGraw-Hill, 1972.

MacLeod, H. "Successful execs don't keep banker's hours." *New York Post,* September 28, 1977, p. 35.

Marcus, S. *Minding the Store.* New York: New American Library, 1974.

Martin, P.R. (Ed.) *The Possible Dream: How 23 Top Executives Live, Work and Play.* Princeton: Dow-Jones, 1975.

Mattlin, E. "How not to be no. 1 without even trying." *The New York Times,* June 5, 1974, p. 43.

"McCall's World," *McCall's,* September 1978, p. 2.

McClelland, D. *The Achieving Society.* Princeton: Van Nostrand, 1961.

McClelland, D., J. Atkinson, R. Clark, and E. Lowell. *The Achievement Motive.* New York: Appleton-Century-Crofts, 1953.

McClelland, D., and D.H. Burnham. "Power is the great motivator." *Harvard Business Review*, March-April 1976, pp. 100–110.

McLean, A.A. (Ed.) *Occupational Stress*. Springfield: Chas. C. Thomas, 1974.

———. *To Work Is Human*. New York: Macmillan, 1967.

———. *Work Stress*. Reading, MA: Addison-Wesley, 1979.

McMurry, R.N. "The executive neurosis." *Harvard Business Review*, November-December 1952, p. 33.

McPherson, M. *The Power Lovers*. New York: Putnam, 1975.

Mead, S. *How To Succeed in Business Without Really Trying*. New York: Simon & Schuster, 1952.

Meineker, R.L. "Dependency and work conflict." In *To Work Is Human*, ed. by A.A. McLean. New York: Macmillan, 1967.

Menninger, W. "If you're a 'workaholic,' you won't read this." *The Philadelphia Inquirer*, December 28, 1975, p. 1-H.

Merry, R. "Labor letter." *The Wall Street Journal*, February 2, 1971, p. 1.

Merton, R.K., M. Fiske, and P.L. Kendall. *The Focused Interview*. Glencoe, IL: The Free Press, 1956.

Meyer, H.E. "The boss ought to take more time off." *Fortune*, June 1974, p. 140.

Mintzberg, H. *The Nature of Managerial Work*. New York: Harper & Row, 1973.

Moramarco, S.S. "What you should know about yourself in a job interview." *Redbook*, September 1979, p. 50.

Morse, N., and R. Weiss. "The function and meaning of work and the job." *American Sociological Review* 20–2(1955):191–198.

Mossesson, B.K. "Your work and your sex life: For better or worse." *Working Woman*, October 1977, p. 62.

Muinzer, G. "Alumni profile." *Princeton Alumni Weekly*, October 18, 1976, p. 12.

"Music's charms may lengthen life." *The New York Times*, December 5, 1978, p. C1.

Nightingale, B. "Frost's bite is back on TV." *US*, June 13, 1978, p. 26.

"Nobel laureate from the Bronx gives medicine its most sensitive chemical detector." *People*, December 26, 1977, p. 95.

Norbom, M.A. "Are you working too hard?" *Dynamic Years*, September–October 1979, p. 35.

Nord, W.R. "Job satisfaction reconsidered." *American Psychologist*, December 1977, p. 1026.

Norman, L.E. "Live a little." *The New York Times*, March 22, 1976, p. 25.

"Not much time for anything but work." *Business Week*, May 4, 1974, p. 70.

Oates, J.C. "Why work isn't work to Joyce Carol Oates." *The New York Times*, March 30, 1975, Sec. 1, p. 38.

Oates, W.E. *Confessions of a Workaholic*. New York: Abingdon Press, 1971.

———. *Workaholics, Make Laziness Work for You*. Garden City: Doubleday, 1978.

Oberndorf, C.P. "Psychopathology of work." *Bulletin of The Menninger Clinic* 15(1951):77–84.

O'Brien, P. "Washington works to cure workaholics." *The Philadelphia Inquirer*, April 15, 1979, p. 8E.

Odiorne, G.S. *Management and the Activity Trap*. New York: Harper & Row, 1974.

Ordine, B. "Dick Vermeil: What will he do to win?" *Today* [Philadelphia Inquirer], November 18, 1979, p. 16.

O'Reilly, C.A., III. "Personality-job fit: Implications for individual attitudes and performance." *Organizational Behavior and Human Performance* 18(1977):36–46.

Orzack, L. "Work as a 'central life interest' of professionals." *Social Problems* 7(2)(1959)125–132.

Osgood, C. "Newsbreak." *CBS News*, February 8, 1977.

Parker, S. *The future of Work and Leisure*. New York: Praeger, 1971.

Patchen, M. *Participation, Achievement and Involvement on the Job*. Englewood Cliffs: Prentice-Hall, 1970.

Peele, S. "Addiction: The analgesic experience." *Human Nature*, September 1978, pp. 61–67.

Peer, E. "Barbara Walters: Star of the Morning." *Newsweek*, May 6, 1974, p. 56.

———. "She spoke her mind." *Newsweek*, November 27, 1978, p. 75.

———. "The work junkies." *Newsweek*, October 8, 1979, p. 87.

"People," *Time*, November 29, 1976, p. 75.

Pesman, S. "Workaholics: Pushing to avoid frustrations of marriage." *The Washington Post*, May 19, 1974, p. L1.

"Physician says stress can be good or not good." *The New York Times*, October 16, 1977, p. 15.

Polykoff, S. *Does She . . . or Doesn't She?* Garden City: Doubleday, 1975.

Porter, L.W., E.E. Lawler, III. and J.R. Hackman. *Behavior in Organizations*. New York: McGraw-Hill, 1975.

Powledge, T.M. "Retirement, one of the hardest jobs in America." *The New York Times*, December 21, 1975, Sec. 5, p. 14.

Price, B.D. "Running with the readers." *Princeton Alumni Weekly*, May 21, 1979, p. 14.

Pym, D. "Better working lives? A personal viewpoint." *Occupational Psychology* 47(1973):33–36.

Rabinowitz, S., and D.T. Hall. "Organizational research on job involvement." *Psychological Bulletin* 84(2)(1977):265–288.

Rabinowitz, S., D.T. Hall, and J.G. Goodale. "Job scope and individual differences as predictors of job involvement: Independent or interactive?" *Academy of Management Journal,* June 1977, pp. 273–281.

Rapoport, R., and R. Rapoport. "Work and family in contemporary society." *American Sociological Review.* 30(3), 381–394.

Reeves, R. "Richard Reeves on Political Books." *The Washington Monthly,* October 1977, p. 57.

Richman, A. "For the afflicted, a champion in court." *The New York Times,* April 25, 1979, p. B1.

Riesman, D. *The Lonely Crowd.* New Haven: Yale University Press, 1950.

Roberts, K. *Leisure.* London: Longman, 1970.

Robinson, D. *The Miracle Finders.* New York: McKay, 1976.

Robinson, J. "The real Barbara Walters." *Vogue,* September 1978, p. 504.

Rogers, J.E. "Working yourself sick." *Mademoiselle,* September 1977, p. 58.

Romo, J.M., P. Siltanen, T. Theorell, and R.H. Rahe. "Work behavior, time urgency and life dissatisfactions in subjects with myocardial infarction: A cross-cultural study." *Journal of Psychosomatic Research* 18–1(1974):1–8.

Rooney, A.A. "A nation of workaholics." *The Chicago Tribune,* September 4, 1977, Sec. 2, p. 1.

Rosenbaum, J. "Are you a workaholic?" *Family Weekly,* March 25, 1979, p. 11.

Rosenblum, C. "Are you addicted to work?" *The Daily News,* June 24, 1979, p. 3.

Rosene, M. "When executives go out on their own." *Venture,* October 1979, p. 55.

Rosow, J.M. (Ed.) *The Worker and the Job.* New York: The American Assembly, 1974.

Salzman, L. *The Obsessive Personality.* New York: Science House, 1968.

Santayana, G. *Character and Opinion in the United States.* New York: Norton, 1967.

Sarason, S.B. *Work, Aging, and Social Change.* New York: Free Press, 1977.

Schaffer, R.H. "The psychological barriers to management effectiveness." *Business Horizons,* April 1971.

Schein, E.H. *Organizational Psychology* (2nd ed.). Englewood Cliffs: Prentice-Hall, 1970.

Schein, V.E., E.H. Maurer, and J.F. Novak. "Impact of flexible working hours on productivity." *Journal of Applied Psychology* 62(4)(1977):463–465.

Schonberg, H. "The city's beat is *allegro furioso.*" *New York Times,* March 21, 1976, Sec. 8, p. 1.

Schoonmaker, A.N. *Anxiety and the Executive.* New York: AMACOM, 1969.

Schrank, R. *Ten Thousand Working Days.* Cambridge: MIT Press, 1978.

Schuyten, P.J. "How MCA rediscovered movieland's golden lode." *Fortune,* November 1976, p. 122.

Schwarzbaum, L. "Failure: The first step to success." *Mademoiselle,* September 1976, p. 178.

Seidenberg, R. *Corporate Wives—Corporate Casualties?* New York: AMACOM, 1973.

Shabecoff, P. "A right to work for the aging class." *The New York Times,* July 17, 1977, Sec. 4, p. 10.

Shapiro, D. *Neurotic Styles.* New York: Basic Books, 1965.

Shapiro, S.A., and A.J. Tuckman. *Time Off: A Psychological Guide to Vacations.* Garden City: Doubleday, 1978.

Shearer, L. "Seven-day workweek." *Parade,* November 2, 1975, p. 4.

Sheehy, G. *Passages.* New York: Dutton, 1976.

Sheridan, J.H. "Do more, work less." *Industry Week,* April 17, 1978, p. 59.

Shimmin, S. "Concepts of work." *Occupational Psychology* 40(1966):195–201.

Shook, R.L., and R. Bingaman. *Total Commitment.* New York: Frederick Fell, 1975.

Sifford, D. "Workaholism: A social disease attacking marriages." *The Philadelphia Inquirer,* October 31, 1976, p. 1M.

————. "You don't need to feel so guilty about having fun." *The Philadelphia Inquirer,* January 15, 1978, p. 1H.

Simon, R.J. "Work habits of eminent scholars." *Sociology of Work and Occupations* 1(3)(1974):327.

Slagle, A. "The instant millionaires." *Daily News,* April 8, 1979, p. 5.

Sloane, L. "Merchant chief at the big board." *The New York Times,* November 14, 1976, Sec. 3, p. 7.

Slobogin, K. "Stress." *The New York Times Magazine,* November 20, 1977, p. 48.

Smilgis, M. "What makes Rather run 110 hours a week? Dapper Dan denies it's for Cronkite's throne." *People,* September 5, 1977, p. 56.

Smith, P.C., L.M. Kendall, and C.L. Hulin. *The Measurement of Satisfaction in Work and Retirement.* Chicago: Rand McNally, 1969.

Sofer, C. *Men in Mid-Career.* Cambridge, UK: The University Press, 1970.

Special Task Force to the Secretary of Health, Education and Welfare. *Work in America.* Cambridge: MIT Press, 1973.

Sprague, P.F. *What Do You Do for a Living?* Princeton: Dow-Jones, 1975.

Staines, G.L., and R.P. Quinn, "American workers evaluate the quality of their jobs." *Monthly Labor Review,* January 1979, p. 3.

Steiner, J. "What price success?" *Harvard Business Review,* March-April, 1972, p. 69.

Stevens, C. "Your mind, your body." *Working Woman,* p. 23.

Suojanen, W.W., and D.R. Hudson. "Coping with stress and addictive work behavior." *Atlanta Economic Review,* March-April 1977, p. 4.

Tarrant, J.J. *Drucker: The Man Who Invented the Corporate Society.* Boston: Cahners, 1976.
Taylor, G.C. "Executive stress." In *To Work Is Human,* ed. by A.A. McLean. New York: Macmillan, 1967.
Terhune, W.B. "Brief psychotherapy with executives in industry: The emotional checkup." In *Progress in Psychotherapy.* New York: Grune & Stratton, Vol. 5, 1960, pp. 132–139.
Terkel, S. *Working.* New York: Avon, 1974.
Theroux, P. "Where's daddy? The life of the Washington workaholic." *The Washingtonian,* December 1974, pp. 92–97.
Tobias, A. "Charles Revson: A remembrance of fire and ice." *New York,* September 8, 1975, p. 39.
Toffler, A. *Future Shock.* New York: Bantam, 1970.

Ullman, L. *Changing.* New York: Knopf, 1977.
Upson, N. *How To Survive as a Corporate Wife.* Garden City: Doubleday, 1974.
Uris, A. *The Efficient Executive.* New York: McGraw-Hill, 1957.

Vaillant, G. *Adaptation to Life.* Boston: Little, Brown, 1977.
Vandervelde, M. "The corporate wife." *Across the Board,* March 1979, p. 21.
Vecsey, G. "A supersalesman turns from vacuum cleaners to homeless pets." *The New York Times,* February 19, 1976, p. 39.

"A visitor's guide to . . . the new Washington." *Business Week,* January 8, 1979, p. 92.

Warr, P., and T. Wall. *Work and Well-Being.* UK: Penguin, 1975.

Weber, M. *The Protestant Ethic and the Spirit of Capitalism.* 1904. Translated by T. Parsons. New York: Scribner's, 1958.

Weick, K.E. "The management of stress." *MBA,* October 1975, p. 37.

Weintraub, J.R. "The relationship between job satisfaction and psychosomatic disorders." Paper presented at Western Psychological Association Convention, April 1975.

White, K. "The woman executive." *Sky,* August 1979, p. 50.

White, R.W. (Ed.) *The Study of Lives.* Chicago: Aldine, 1963.

Wiener, Y., and A.S. Gechman. "Commitment: A behavioral approach to job involvement." Paper presented at the meeting of the Academy of Management, New Orleans, August 1975.

Wilensky, H.L. "The uneven distribution of leisure: The impact of economic growth on 'free time'." *Social Problems* 9(1)(1961):32–56.

————. "Varieties of work experience." In *Man in a World at Work,* ed. by H. Borow. Boston: Houghton Mifflin, 1964.

Williams, R.S., P.C. Morea, and J.M. Ives. "The significance of work: An empirical study." *Journal of Occupational Psychology* 48(1975):45–51.

Williams, W. "City power crisis musters executive grit and muscle." *The New York Times,* July 15, 1977, p. D3.

Willmot, P. "Family, work and leisure conflicts among

male employees." *Human Relations* 24(6)(1971): 575–584.

Wilson, E.Z. "Addicted to work." *Glamour*, December 1979, p. 198.

Wilson, S. *The Man in the Gray Flannel Suit.* New York: Simon & Schuster, 1955.

Wolfe, T. *You Can't Go Home Again.* New York: Grosset & Dunlap, 1940.

Wolman, B.B. *Victims of Success.* New York: Quadrangle, 1973.

"Women and success—why some find it so painful." *The New York Times,* January 28, 1978, p. 14.

Wooten, J. *Dasher.* New York: Summit Books, 1978.

Wyse, L. *Mrs. Success.* New York: World, 1970.

Yenckel, J.T. "Careers: working for a workaholic." *The Washington Post,* October 31, 1979, p. B5.

"Young top management: The new goals, rewards, life-styles." *Business Week,* October 6, 1975, p. 56.

Zaleznik, A., and M.F.R. Kets de Vries. *Power and the Corporate Mind.* Boston: Houghton Mifflin, 1975.

Zuckerman, M. "The search for high sensation." *Psychology Today,* February 1978, p. 38.

Zuckerman, M., E.A. Kolin, L. Price, and I. Zoob. "Development of a sensation-seeking scale." *Journal of Consulting Psychology,* 28(6)(1964):477–482.

Index